To my older
best friend and
continue to sharpen you
as of "iron sharpens iron,
so one man sharpens another"

Rob Paterson
August 2000

MIGHTY MAN OF GOD

SAM LAING

MIGHTY MAN OF GOD

A Return to the Glory of Manhood

DPI

DISCIPLESHIP
PUBLICATIONS
INTERNATIONAL

Cover design: Chris Costello
Interior design: Ladislao Mandiola and Chad Crossland

ISBN: 1-57782-118-1

To Mitch Mitchell
and the Mighty Men of
the Triangle Church:

Brave warriors, all.
Forever my friends.

Contents

ACKNOWLEDGMENTS

My daughter Elizabeth gave large amounts of her time and considerable amounts of her prodigious literary ability in helping me with this book. Her editorial skills, creative suggestions and encouraging spirit have done much to enable my efforts to come to fruition. And, since during this time she was in the throes of preparing for her upcoming wedding, it makes her contributions all the more appreciated. Elizabeth and I share a common love of writing, of words and of language, and the time we spent together working on this book will always be to me a precious memory.

My good friend Mitch Mitchell compiled the information used to tell the tale of the deeds of the Mighty Men of the Triangle Church.

Tracy MacLachlan, my devoted, skilled and talented assistant, helped me throughout this project. Especially did she assist me in battling my computer, first to a draw and finally into some degree of submission.

My thanks as always go out in fullest measure to my friends at DPI. Tom Jones is one of the most courageous, heroic and devoted men I know—a true mighty man of God.

To my beloved wife, family and church, thank you for your patience and encouragement. I am looking forward to renewing our acquaintance. I have missed you very much.

To Mozart, Bach, Govi, Oscar Lopez, Philip Lester, Kevin Darby, the Chieftains, the Wind Machine, the Gypsy Kings, Marc Antoine, Peter Krater and the guitarists of Windham Hill and Higher Octave Music, thank you for the sweet sounds that kept me writing, thinking and creating through many long and lonely hours.

INTRODUCTION

"They were brave warriors, ready for battle and able to handle the shield and spear. Their faces were the faces of lions, and they were as swift as gazelles in the mountains" (1 Chronicles 12:8).

You are invited to a special meeting on Saturday, October 10 at 5:30 AM at the Triangle Church. I have some plans to present that will change your life and have a profound influence on the entire church. The inconvenience of the hour is by design. If you do not wholeheartedly desire to be there, please do not come. If you are late, turn around and go home. The doors will be locked at the beginning of the meeting and will not be opened until we finish one hour later.

The meeting will be with a handpicked group of men. I believe one of the greatest needs in the kingdom of God today is for the men to rise up and become like the great men of God we read about in the Bible. This meeting will give you the challenge and direction to change your life and go places spiritually you have never been before. I request that you talk about this meeting only on a need-to-know basis. For example, you may need to tell your wife or roommates where you are going, but I expect there to be no chatter or idle conversation. I want you, and this group, to be felt by deeds, and not by words.

Read, study, and meditate upon 1 Chronicles 11 and 12 and 2 Samuel 23:8-39 in preparation.

(signed) Sam Laing

It was with this letter that a powerful movement among the men of my church was begun. I met with twenty-nine men that morning and challenged them to become "mighty men of God," men like those brave warriors of David's day, powerful men who made a difference. We talked about the sad condition

9

of manhood in our world and about the failure of men even in the kingdom of God to be real men, and we decided we wanted to do something about it. In this meeting I urged the group to excel in seven areas that are elaborated upon in the appendix.

We Band of Brothers

David's mighty men were the inspiration for the Mighty Men of the Triangle Church and for this book. Look at the words that appear in the verses describing those men: *Warriors. Ready. Brave. Able. Prepared. Leaders. Commanders. Undividedly loyal. Experienced. Fully determined. Of one mind. Volunteers for service. Ready for battle. Brave young warriors. Men who understood the times. Exploits. Great exploits. Honored. Doubly honored. Famous. Greater honor. Valiant fighters. They took their stand. Great victory. Risked their lives. Blood. Joy in Israel. For the sake of his people Israel.* But someone will say, "This is from the Old Testament. This does not sound like Jesus. This is about war, killing and violence. How can this apply to men in today's church, men who are committed to being humble, to turning the other cheek, to being kind and merciful?"

The answer to this question is actually not that difficult to figure out. The New Testament teaches us that we too are in a war—not a war for territory or for political or economic power, but a spiritual war. This is a war for our own souls, for the souls of our families, and for the souls of men and women all over the world. It is a battle much more important and much more intense than any Old Testament conflict. Our enemy is not an army of flesh and blood; it is the army of the angels of Satan himself. In this conflict we are called to be soldiers, to put on our armor and to fight the good fight of the faith (Ephesians 6:10-20; 1 Timothy 1:18, 6:12; 2 Timothy 4:7). If we, as a church, are to win this war, we must rekindle the warrior spirit in God's people. And most important of all, *it must be rekindled in the hearts of our men.*

Radical Change

But back to our story. I did not know how the men would respond that morning, or what the results would be in their lives; I only knew that something needed to be done, that something needed to happen to get the men of my church to become the powerful, godly men I read about in the Bible.

I was inspired, amazed—no—*stunned* by what happened to the men in that room that day and in the months following. It was as if a fire was lit, as if chains were torn away, as if something deep and primeval in these men's hearts had been touched, as if a part of their souls awoke that had long been sleeping. They sat up straighter in their chairs. They leaned forward to hear. Their eyes gleamed with desire; there was a fire kindled in their hearts. To a man, they responded to what they heard with joy, zeal and longing. *They became better men by the mere fact of being challenged.* They left the room that day walking taller, smiling brighter and laughing louder. They set about their goals with a vengeance. They did mighty deeds, accomplished amazing exploits and made powerful changes in their lives.

In subsequent meetings they have come back together and shared the great victories God has continued to give them as they strive to bring him glory by doing, and being, more. I am committed to this group and its purposes as a major focus of my efforts in building my congregation. The results have been too dramatic for me to do otherwise. We will continue to meet, to grow, to change, to become what we dream we can be and to do what we believe we must. We want to be mighty men of God!

The Sobering Truth

The condition of manhood in our world is deplorable. Men are viewed as superficial, shallow louts. A goofy, foolish object of pity, the masculine gender is the butt of countless jokes and subject to an endless stream of ridicule. When was the last time you saw a man portrayed as a hero, as a person of dignity, honor and grace? Of noble and sacrificial virtue? No, the picture is one of a lustful, vulgar vagabond who neither wants, nor is capable of, real friendship and commitment. Devoid of love and loyalty, men are represented as without real friendships with one another and without allegiance to women and children. Power hungry, brutish, violent, greedy, sports obsessed, conniving, lazy, aloof, cowardly, depressed...need I go on? And this is the being created in the image of God, who was given care and dominion over God's creation, who was told that he was a little lower than the angels! We can only join with David as he lamented the demise of a great man in his life by saying, "Your glory...lies slain on your heights. How the mighty have fallen!" (2 Samuel 1:19).

As men, we must admit with shame that there is a very real basis for these charges. We have failed to be what we should be; we are guilty of every one of these accusations—and worse. If a gender can be indicted for its crimes, then as men we must all together hang our heads and cry out, "Guilty as charged!"

Sometimes I think the women of the world, with God joining them, must ask themselves the question, *Where are the men?* Where are the men who will marry women and stay with them, faithful until death? Where are the men who will love their wives and stand beside them to raise the children and build a family? Where are the men who will lead our nations and guide our governments with wisdom and dignity? It seems like men of the courage, honor and eloquence of a Lincoln or a Churchill are no more. The presidents and leaders of today seem unable to remain faithful to their own wives, much less inspire a nation to greatness.

Where are the men of God's kingdom? Where are the men to lead the way in evangelism, in prayer, in love and in faith? Is it not the women who so often set the pace in spirituality, in numerical growth and in hearts devoted to God? Where are the men to marry the thronging crowds of single women in our churches? Are the single brothers in our fellowship mired in the same morass of selfishness and immaturity as the men in the world around them? Where are the men who could rise up and be leaders in our churches? Are they too wrapped up in their own pursuits, too concerned with making money and being comfortable? Where are the great heroes of faith we need to inspire our teens and our college students and to inspire us all? We call out for them, and sometimes it seems there are no men out there to answer our cries.

Wake Up!

I believe the true men are out there. I know they are! I believe some of them are reading this book. You may have been sleeping the sleep of selfishness, or chained in the bonds of fear, or locked in the prison of low vision, but I believe you are out there. I believe you are waiting to hear the call of God, the call to the glory of manhood, the call to rise up, the call to run and not grow weary, to soar on eagle's wings.

This book is a call for you to ascend to the heights of dignity and nobility that God intended for you when he made you. It is a call to forsake the paths of selfishness and vulgarity and become a hero who thinks of himself last and others first. It is a call to grow, to change, to step out and step up. It is a call to greatness, to be free of the chains of pride, fear and sensuality that have too long bound you. It is a call to conquer your weaknesses and fears, to leave them forever in your past as you forge onward and upward to your true destiny—to become a mighty man of God!

Sam Laing
Bald Head Island, North Carolina
February 1999

PART 1

THE FOUNDATIONS
OF MANHOOD

SPIRITUALITY

The spiritual man makes judgments about all things, but he himself is not subject to any man's judgment:

*"For who has known the mind of the Lord
    that he may instruct him?"*

But we have the mind of Christ.

1 Corinthians 2:15-16

One cannot be a mighty man of God without being a spiritual man. It is spirituality that gives us our power. Spirituality is the mysterious quality that imparts to our lives a unique dimension that sets us apart. Being a spiritual man is about depending on the power of God. If we reach for the stars but rely on ourselves, we will fall back to earth exhausted, defeated and discouraged. It is spirituality that will take us to the heights, that will enable us to radically and permanently change.

A man can be no mightier than his relationship with God allows. If then we want to be mighty men of God, we must seek to know God, to love him and to be his friends. We cannot come to God for power, strength and transformation and neglect being close to him. He does not give his gifts for our own use or on our terms, but for his glory and in his way.

Depth

Many of us are focused on *doing,* not on *being.* We want to work, accomplish and achieve for God, but we do not desire to draw near to God and deal with our inner selves. Venturing into the deep waters frightens us, so we wade in the shallows. We do not think deeply, feel deeply or love deeply. We are lightweights. Others sense that we are just actors, putting on a show. We lack depth, and it shows in every aspect of our lives.

We cannot talk to our wives because we are shallow. We lack influence with our children because we are shallow. We lack deep friendships because we are shallow. We cannot express ourselves, and have little to say when we do, because we are shallow. When we have much to say, our words fall to the ground anyway, because we are shallow. We do not change, or do not change for long, because we are shallow. We are lonely, depressed, discouraged and empty because we are shallow. We are weak men, not mighty men, because *we are shallow!*

But God did not make us shallow. He made us with hearts that can feel, think and be. He made us like himself. We have minds, souls and spirits. We are more than machines—we are *men.* The problem is not that we are fundamentally flawed; the problem is that we will not deepen ourselves. We will not let ourselves go beyond the surface. We prefer to keep things on a superficial level because we fear what we, or others, might find if we went deeper. We seek to avoid pain and instead choose a lifetime of aching emptiness. We seek to avoid embarrassment and instead find the isolation that pride brings. We seek to protect ourselves with shallowness but it becomes the instrument of our destruction.

God works from the inside out. God looks at who you really are, not what you appear to be. As he selected the next king to lead his people, he told the prophet Samuel,

> *"Do not consider his appearance or his height, for I have rejected him. The Lord does not look at the things man looks at. Man looks at the outward appearance, but the Lord looks at the heart." (1 Samuel 16:7)*

David, the leader of the mighty men, was preeminently a man of heart, of spirituality. David was a man who loved God in a deeply personal way. He prayed. He sang songs of worship; he poured out his heart. The psalms he wrote continue to live on thousands of years later because they speak of a relationship with God that we all long for. David's spirituality was the secret of his almost magical power of leadership. His men were fiercely loyal to him and gave him their complete trust because they knew he was a spiritual man, a man who walked with God.

Consistent Study

First, a spiritual man is a man of God's word. We must become men who take God's word into our deepest selves. The Bible is a double-edged sword that is meant to penetrate to the depths of our souls. Yet for many of us, being cut to the heart is but a distant memory from the days of our conversion. We now have hard, tired, dull hearts that have lost the sense of awe of God's love and holiness. How can we make our hearts tender again? It will take effort, the effort of intense, regular, personal Bible study. It will mean getting out our Bibles and begging God to speak to us from them once again. It will mean taking notes, agonizing over passages and letting them apply to our lives as we did in the past. It will mean spending more than a few minutes a day studying—it will mean carving out more time in our schedules and devoting some late nights, early mornings, half-days and whole days to digging into the Word.

It will mean committing God's word to memory. One of the challenges I gave our Mighty Man group in Triangle was to commit chapters and sections of the Bible to memory. My sons memorized the entire book of 2 Timothy. As they recited it before one of our meetings, the men present were moved to tears. What an incredible effort, and what an incredible reward all of us reaped from it!

Devoted Prayer

A spiritual man is devoted to prayer (Colossians 4:2). This will mean getting up early like Jesus did so that you can pray undisturbed before you start your day. It will involve going to a quiet place to pray, where you are completely alone and can pour out your soul to God. It may entail going to the private room that Jesus talked about (Matthew 6:6) or someplace outdoors. It will mean taking some time to get away by yourself, all alone, so that you can pray more fervently. It will mean learning to pray out loud. It will call for praying on your knees and with your hands raised to heaven. It will include praying with a loud voice and with tears. It will require learning to pray constantly, bringing God into the details of your everyday life. It will take everything we have got and more! But the rewards of being a spiritual man are too great—we cannot back away from the challenge!

Most of us bear more sorrow, more anxiety and burdens than we know. We worry about our families, our finances and our futures. We go through life nagged constantly by unsettling anxiety. We need to learn to cast all of our burdens, from the most weighty to the most mundane, upon our loving Father in heaven. We cannot do this in an offhanded, cursory manner. It is going to take real effort. For most of us, this will mean that the amount and quality of personal time with God that we have been spending is going to have to significantly increase.

Continual Growth

Some of us are at the same place in our relationship with God where we were years ago. No wonder we are shallow! We are still living at the level of a spiritual infant. We are still worldly and unspiritual because we have not progressed beyond our early days as Christians. Our prayer lives, Bible study and depth of communion with God are static, yet our lives have only become more complicated and challenging as time has gone by. We read the same verses, spend the same amount of time and follow the same spiritual routine day in and day out. Some of us may even desire to be closer to God but are too lazy to put in the effort. It is our laziness that is stunting our spiritual growth and leaving us sadly deficient in spirituality. We must go further, take more time and take it deeper than we ever have before if we are to become mighty men of God.

Men, we are talking about a *relationship* here. Your friendship with God is either getting deeper, or it is dying. It cannot be set up, then put on hold or in a cruise-control mode. Imagine taking that same attitude with your wife. Imagine being married for years, but never coming to know each other any better, never getting closer. What an empty shell of a marriage that would be! Yet that is just what many of us men have done with God. We think, *Okay, I'm saved, so I have my relationship with God covered. Now let me go on and do something else.* It just doesn't work that way! Relationships need to grow, and to grow they must be nurtured.

Begin today. Decide that you are going to seek to know God, to draw nearer to him than ever before. Repent of your unspiritual, superficial devotion. Then decide that you will spend some extra time with God. I would urge you as soon as possible to take at least one night and day and get away completely by yourself. Fast if you need to. Do as the mighty men of the Bible did—spend time alone with God, in large quantities, as often as you need it. Develop consistency in your daily devotions. Learn to pour your heart out in prayer, and open your heart to God's word. Decide that your relationship with God will begin anew and that you will never again allow it to become stagnant or dull. Decide that every day you will fight to grow closer to God, no matter what the cost—and watch as you experience a spiritual glory and joy that David wrote about:

O God, you are my God,
  earnestly I seek you;
my soul thirsts for you,
  my body longs for you,
in a dry and weary land
  where there is no water.
I have seen you in the sanctuary
  and beheld your power and your glory.
Because your love is better than life,
  my lips will glorify you.
I will praise you as long as I live,
  and in your name I will lift up my hands.
My soul will be satisfied as with the richest of foods;
  with singing lips my mouth will praise you. (Psalm 63:1-5)

2

Humility

"I am gentle and humble in heart."

Matthew 11:29

Jesus, the greatest man who ever lived, described himself as humble in heart. Of all the descriptions he could have given himself, he chose this one. If we are to become mighty men, we must be like Jesus. And if we are to be like Jesus, we must become humble.

All the great men of the Bible were humble. It was said of Moses that he was "a very humble man, more humble than anyone else on the face of the earth" (Numbers 12:3). Pride is the greatest sin of men. It is the root sin behind every other that we commit and is the true culprit behind every masculine weakness detailed in this book. Behind every failure in your life, look for the sin of pride—you will always find it somewhere, either lurking in the shadows or strutting about in broad daylight. Every man struggles with pride, from the most obviously arrogant and conceited man to the man who seems to have no confidence at all—all of us are guilty of this terrible sin. To become mighty men, we must first deal with our pride. We must admit that we are not mighty men and that we can never become mighty but by the power of God.

A Sense of Need

Humility can be defined as having a *sense of need*. We must first admit our need for God. We need his love. We need his power. We need his forgiveness. We need his companionship.

Jesus said, "By myself I can do nothing..." (John 5:30). If Jesus, who was the son of God, said he could do nothing apart from God, how much greater is our need!

Not only do we need God, but we need other people as well. God, in his wisdom, has placed us in his church, the body of Christ. As members of a body, we are dependent upon the other members of that body. We cannot function all alone. We are headed for disaster if we take the attitude, "It's just me and God, and I don't need anyone else." Such an attitude is the height of pride and is an offense to God.

Most men fail miserably in letting other people know their deepest needs. We have the foolish, mistaken idea that to be strong we must pretend that we have no problems. We think it is weak and wimpy to let other people know that we don't have it all together, that we have areas of our lives in which we feel hopelessly inadequate and insecure. For example we won't let our wives "in" to talk to us about our true thoughts and feelings. They long for a closer relationship with us and see us struggling with problems, but we won't let them be our best friends. We won't let other men inside either. We feel we would lose their respect if they knew what we were really like. The truth is, most men would love to have a friend with whom they could be completely honest! Because we are so closed, we become incredibly lonely. This situation can worsen as the years progress until we one day find ourselves completely alone, shut down and isolated.

A humble man not only admits his need, he admits his sins. The Bible teaches us that "if we claim to be without sin, we deceive ourselves and the truth is not in us" (1 John 1:8). We are also told in the Scriptures that we should "confess [our] sins to each other and pray for each other" (James 5:16). We should be deeply aware of our sins before God and be open about them with the people around us. Being a mighty man does not mean that we pretend to be perfect. Some men, in an attempt to appear strong and powerful, act as if they can do no wrong. How foolish and how far from the picture of the strong man presented in the Bible!

We men have a terrible time admitting when we are wrong— we don't even like to admit it to ourselves. We would rather make excuses than to simply admit we have failed or made a mistake. We especially don't like to admit our sins to our wives. We would rather ignore the problem, put the blame on them, or criticize them for being overly sensitive than to admit our wrongdoings. As a result, we frustrate and embitter our wives, destroying the love we once had. Furthermore, we don't like to admit our failings to other men. We want to keep up a macho image with other guys, and we think if we admitted to any sins or mistakes that we would forfeit their esteem. It is not difficult to see the result—we are lonely and have few intimate friends because in our pride we will not let other men into our inner life.

Humility also admits its weaknesses. The strength of the mighty man comes through his open admission of weakness. It is only then that he can draw upon the great power of God. Paul was a proud man before he became a Christian. God humbled him when he became a disciple, but he still struggled with pride later in life. He tells us that he was even tempted to become conceited because of the great revelations that God showed him as an apostle. But God humbled Paul again by giving him a weakness, a "thorn in [the] flesh" (2 Corinthians 12:7). Paul said that on three different occasions he begged God to take away his weakness, but that at the end of his praying, the answer was, "'My grace is sufficient for you, for my power is made perfect in weakness'" (2 Corinthians 12:9). God's mighty strength becomes ours when we, like Paul, humbly confess before God and man our weaknesses.

Characteristics of Humility

A humble man is *approachable*. He does not leave the impression that he is too proud to be questioned or challenged. The way of approach is open, not only to those who are his peers or superiors, but also to those he leads. This means that the wife and children of a humble man feel that they can talk with him about delicate or difficult matters, even those that involve discussing a mistake he may have made, without fear of an angry response.

A humble man will *apologize* when he is wrong. The humble man's attitude is rooted in his deep realization that he falls short of God's standards. His humility will carry him to the point of saying he is sorry to anyone he has hurt or let down—his wife, children, friends—anyone at all. The humble man does not have to be driven into a corner with irrefutable logic to admit his mistakes. He is eager to see them and to see them quickly.

The humble man is *confident*. Because he has nothing to prove and nothing to hide, there is no more confident man on the face of the earth! His confidence is in God and in God's power and not in himself. He is confident *about* himself, but not *in* himself. Like Paul, he says,

> Therefore I will boast all the more gladly about my weaknesses, so that Christ's power may rest on me...I delight in weaknesses...For when I am weak, then I am strong. (2 Corinthians 12:9-10)

A Personal Lesson from God

We are urged in the Scriptures to humble ourselves, but it seems that sometimes God takes a personal interest in our humility. And in my case, I can affirm that not only does he take an interest, but he takes a lifelong interest!

When I was a senior in college, I decided to run for the presidency of our church campus ministry group. I had already served as president during my sophomore year and felt certain that I would be elected again. Running against me were two of my best friends, Bruce Williams and Tom Brown. Bruce was one year younger than me, and Tom was only a sophomore. In my pride I thought that surely the students would have the wisdom to elect the wiser and more mature older brother—me!

As the results came in that fateful night, it became clear that Bruce had defeated me. I was surprised and disappointed but figured that I could easily be elected vice president and still serve as an officer. To my shock and amazement, I lost again. I lost to Tom Brown, the young, brash sophomore. I couldn't believe it! I was stunned and hurt at the same time. After I fought back the tears during the closing song at church, the campus minister, Chuck Lucas, seeing my condition, pulled me aside and said something I would never forget: "I guess now we'll see whether you're in it for your own glory or the glory of God." His words exposed my pride and brought me down to earth. I went home that night and resolved that I would have the greatest year of my Christian life and that instead of feeling sorry for myself, I would be a servant to our student group and to our new officers. I went on to have an outstanding year of spiritual growth, and I had learned a great lesson.

At least I thought I had. Almost twenty years later I moved to Boston, Massachusetts, with my family to receive further training in the ministry. Leading the church there was Kip McKean, a man five years younger than I whom I had helped bring into the church when he was a freshman in my fraternity. Making the decision to move and receive training from someone whom I had first invited to church was humbling enough, but there was more humility to come.

When I arrived in Boston, Kip quickly informed me that I would be serving as a house church leader under none other than Tom Brown! I was surprised and disappointed but decided that I would make the best of the situation and serve as Tom's righthand man. Then Kip informed me that I would not be serving as Tom's righthand man, but Bruce Williams would!

I was at first shocked and angry. Then, somewhere in the back of my mind, I thought back to that election night almost twenty years before, and I realized the lesson I thought I had learned was being taught to me all over again. I saw that in God's own way and time, he was humbling me again. I also realized that God must have a great sense of humor!

I have since learned to laugh at my foolish pride, but I also realize that, although I think I have come a long way in being more humble, many more lessons await me. I am sure that if Tom, Bruce and I ever make it to the same nursing home, Tom and Bruce will be president and vice president, and I will be in charge of straightening up the rocking chairs!

Do you want to be a man of strength and power, a mighty man? Humble yourself. Humble yourself before God and others. Admit that you need God and that you need people. Admit your sins, weaknesses and failures. Depend on God to help you change. Do not waste your time trying to exalt yourself—the way up is down!

"For whoever exalts himself will be humbled, and whoever humbles himself will be exalted." (Matthew 23:12)

3

COURAGE

Be on your guard; stand firm in the faith; be men of courage; be strong.

1 Corinthians 16:13

Is there any virtue more associated with manhood than courage? Courage is universally admired, praised and sought after. No man who is truly a man does not admire those whom he regards as men of courage.

There are many kinds of courage. We will look at three. We will observe them in the life of King David, the leader of the mighty men.

Courageous Deeds

David, as a teenager, was sent by his father to take food to his older brothers who were fighting for Israel in the army of King Saul. We know the rest of the story—how this young man faced and defeated the giant Goliath, who had reduced an army of brave men to whimpering cowards. David's courage was beyond compare; his deed that day won him a place in our hearts and in the history of God's people forever.

David would probably have looked at us with puzzlement had we rushed up to him that day and breathlessly declared our admiration of his courage. "But this man was insulting God," he would have answered, "What else was there to do?" That is what courage is all about: forgetting ourselves and becoming consumed with the glory of God. Then courage flows in our veins as a matter of course. We do not think about it. We do not think, *I must be courageous now.* We only think, *The name of God, the reputation of his people, the salvation of a soul is at stake. I must act and act quickly!*

The issue of strength for the task is not of concern when we think this way because we know that God will supply whatever we need—because it is his battle to fight and win. We are courageous because we know that God is with us, that God is for us. We are only servants, doing what any servant could and should do in the situation. Thus is born our courage, a courage of true manhood, a courage that inspires those who have been preoccupied with themselves and who have lost sight of God. Do you long for courage? See the world and the battles with the eyes of God, and courage will flow into you as from a mighty river.

Courage to Endure

But there is a courage of another sort, and it in some ways is more difficult, more taxing, more trying than that we have just discussed. It is difficult because the lines of battle are not so clear, and because it is not finished with an afternoon's work.

When David returned to the camp of Saul after his glorious victory over Goliath, he returned with a hero's welcome and to the admiration of all the people. "Saul has slain his thousands," sang the women, "and David his tens of thousands" (1 Samuel 18:7). With that, David was to earn the enmity and brooding jealousy of Saul for the rest of Saul's life. From that day on, Saul considered David his enemy and sought to destroy him. David never knew why this was so, for Saul never spoke of it openly. But act on his jealousy he did, and he drove David from his presence, into the desert as an outlaw and refugee.

God wanted David to remain within the borders of Israel, right under the nose of Saul. David would have preferred to flee to another country (and did so at one time in a moment of cowardice), but God did not allow it. Day after day, month after month, year after year, David and his small band hid from Saul, eking out a hard existence in the barren wastelands of

Judea. This is where David wrote so many of his great psalms, the songs in which he poured out his heart to God, asking him for deliverance, companionship and comfort.

Circumstances like these demand from you courage of a higher order. This is the courage of staying on a righteous course when it seems there is no end to your difficulties, when there is no immediate reward, but only long days of loneliness and hardship. It means keeping up your spirits when there is no end in sight. It is the courage of continuing to trust in God when those who should be encouraging and inspiring you have descended into sin and whose once-exemplary lives have fallen into the dust of pride, worldliness and jealousy. It is the bravery required when your name is dragged down, when you are gossiped about and when your motives are questioned. It is the nerve necessary when you are not sure what you should do, when there are difficulties in your way that do not easily present themselves as right and wrong. It is the courage demanded by the kinds of difficulties you face as you get older, when you see that sometimes, even in God's kingdom, the best people can let you down. This is a courage that must sustain you when you are tested as you have never been tested before.

Courage to Come Back

The third type of courage is that of a man who has failed, who has failed terribly, and who must face his failures and try to find his way back to God, to his true manhood. Once again, the story is familiar—David has committed adultery with Bathsheba and has lied and murdered to cover it up. He must now face the greatest test of his life—does he have the courage to face God, his family, the nation and himself with what he has done? Will he still be a man after the heart of God, or will he throw it all away, now that he has committed such a grievous sin? We see his response, as he recorded it in Psalm 51: he humbled himself, made no excuses, begged God for forgiveness and for a new heart and strove to rebuild his life.

None of us is perfect; we will all sin. Even if we do not sin as tragically as David did, we will sin and then must face the consequences of what we have done. Will we have the courage to cast ourselves on the mercy of God or will we simply run away—or even take our own lives, as did Judas?

But there are other kinds of courage, as well.

Physical courage is the courage we demonstrate when we face danger or death. This is the courage of the soldier, the fireman, the policeman or of any man who is faced with a situation that threatens his physical life. It is what the early Christians faced when they were thrown into the arena. To gain this kind of courage, we simply need to remember that if we are saved and going to heaven, we have nothing to fear—even if it means losing our life.

Emotional courage is the courage required when everything around us seems to be going against us. It is the courage called for when we are under pressure at work, when we have had financial setbacks, or when we are going through spiritual and emotional upheaval. Jesus said that "in this world you will have trouble. But take heart! I have overcome the world" (John 16: 33). Too many of us men are not manly in the way we face adversity. We give in to depression, discouragement and despair. It shows on our faces and in our posture. We are unable to encourage our wives, children and friends. We become a burden rather than a burden-bearer. While it is true that we must learn to express our hurts and fears, we must be careful not to let them dominate us. We must face our fears, but do so with a joyful, manly and confident spirit.

Social courage is the courage to do what is right even when the crowd and popular opinion are against us. It is the courage demonstrated by Jesus when he returned to speak at the synagogue in his home town of Nazareth, only to be received with anger and hostility. This is the courage required of us when we endure persecution for our faith from our families, friends and fellow employees. It is the courage to stand alone with deep conviction and clear vision when all others around us are saying we should compromise. Social courage is required when we must work through difficult issues in relationships. Many of us have conflicts in our marriages and in other important relationships that we will not solve because we are cowards. We are unwilling to speak the truth in love (Ephesians 4:15), and so we remain unreconciled and distanced from those to whom we should be closest. I would urge you, have the courage to have the uncomfortable talks that will free you from the prison of estranged relationships!

Personal courage is the kind of courage required when we challenge ourselves to go where we have never gone before and do what we have never done. This is the bravery demanded of us when we must make a change in our character or in our personality. This is the boldness that will cause us to take a risk rather than to remain comfortable. Many of us are stagnant, dead and bored because we are unwilling to push ourselves beyond our fears. I would urge you to face your fears specifically and take steps to conquer each one.

Motivational courage is seen when God said to Joshua, "Be strong and very courageous. Do not be terrified; do not be discouraged, for the Lord your God will be with you wherever you go" (Joshua 1:9). He meant business! There is a time when a man must simply look his fear in the face and say, "I may be afraid, but I will not let my fear control me." There is a time when, for the sake of God, our families, our manhood and righteousness, we must lay aside our fears, get up on our feet, and march forward to do what is necessary—no matter how we may feel.

Whatever battles you face, face them with God. Whether it is the challenge of an intimidating and boasting wrong that must be righted; whether it is the day-to-day grind of staying strong with God when you are sometimes not sure where he is or what you should do; or whether it is the battle to come back to God when you have grievously sinned, face all of these battles with courage. See them through God's eyes, fight them with his strength, and never, never, *never* give up!

4

Honor

Never pay back evil for evil to anyone. Do things in such a way that everyone can see you are honorable.

Romans 12:17 (NLT)

A mighty man is first and foremost a man of sterling character. He is a good man: a man of the highest principles, of unimpeachable integrity and of unassailable virtue. He is a man of God; he is a man of honor.

An honorable man is one who holds himself to the highest standards or morals, ethics and behavior. This man so conducts his life that he earns the admiration and respect of everyone who knows him. This man is trusted, held in highest esteem, even revered. When he speaks, people listen. He does not have to demand respect; he is freely given it because of his inherent worth. He is admired by the aged and by his peers; he is esteemed by women; he is beloved of children; other men long to be in his presence and seek to emulate his great qualities.

Truth

When Jesus saw Nathanael approaching, he said of him, "Here is a true Israelite, in whom there is nothing false." (John 1:47)

A man of honor is a man of truth. Honesty and loyalty to the truth are the fundamental building blocks of character. Together they form the cornerstone of all that you are and are the North Star of your manhood. All your aspirations, all your hopes, all your dreams for your manhood begin here. Without honesty and truth, we can proceed no further.

When we enter into the presence of Jesus, we sense that we are in the company of a man of pure integrity and honesty. We feel that he is a man of truth, who always keeps his word. He arouses in us undying, unwavering loyalty and confidence because we know he would never deceive us and that he would never lead us astray.

We must *love* the truth. We must love the truth for its own sake. We must so honor the truth that we seek it, embrace it and can bear no departure from it.

We must *believe* the truth. We must accept and receive the truth. We must believe it, no matter what it may cost us or who we may offend. We must seek the truth in God's word and be willing to abandon any notion we hold that is contrary to what God has said.

We must believe the truth about ourselves. Many of us would like to be better, braver and stronger men, but we are unwilling to face who we are. We think of ourselves more highly than we ought. Sometimes we do not see our true selves at all. We blind ourselves to our sins; we rationalize and minimize them. We think others' sins are worse than ours. We may be willing to admit a flaw or weakness, but we do not see our sins in light of the cross, in all of their horror and offensiveness to God. We do not see the offensive behaviors, the character and personality flaws that alienate us from others, rendering us ineffective. Many of us have huge weaknesses that we have never acknowledged or that we do not take very seriously. Our friends and family have to repeatedly bring us to conviction about these things—we do not have a conscience about them. We are blind to them, because we do not love the truth and are unwilling to be men of truth. If we would see ourselves according to the truth, we could change. But because we will not, we remain defeated, isolated and limited men.

We must be willing to *hear* the truth. Many times we cannot see the truth on our own; we need to be told it. The first and worst lie is the one we tell to ourselves. When true words are spoken to us, we need to hear and accept them. They may come in a sermon or in a conversation. The conversation may be with a friend, our wives, our children, with a critic or an enemy—hear the truth! It does not matter who is right; it only matters what is right. Learn to appreciate these moments, however unpleasant they may be—they can be some of the most liberating and freeing times in our lives. Observe the lives of men in moral and spiritual decline, and you will see a pattern of fighting against the truth. Study the lives of men who grow stronger, and you will see men who continually and at crucial moments and junctures of their lives embrace the truth more profoundly.

We must *tell* the truth. We must be men who speak the truth. We must not deceive anyone in any way. Our yes must be yes and our no must be no—absolutely. People must never have reason to doubt our word. We do not have to assure others that on this occasion our word is true, because it always is. On matters great and small, we tell the truth. We do not exaggerate; we do not embellish. We do not make it smaller, larger, bigger, more dramatic. We do not adjust the numbers. We do not take credit that is not ours. We do not deny talent that we possess or claim that which we do not have. We do not excuse ourselves by making up stories. We do not leave a false impression by what we say or do not say. We are not careless with the truth; we are accurate. If we do not know something, we neither say we do nor act as if we do.

Have you ever known someone who simply did not ring true? Something about them is artificial. You always feel that you are getting a revised version of things, not the exact truth. What is your reaction to such people? You do not want to be around them. You feel violated, taken advantage of, and are forever on your guard around them. It is obvious to you that they have no close friends because of their deceit.

The issue of truthfulness is critical to a successful marriage. Our wives must trust us. If we break faith with them, if they feel they cannot absolutely believe our word, we are in for a terrible marriage—a marriage without intimacy, respect or peace. Our wives simply will not be able to give themselves to us emotionally if they do not have confidence in us.

I once had a conversation with a friend who was broken-hearted about his lack of closeness to his wife. With tearful eyes he lamented the coolness and distance between them. As we talked, he freely admitted he struggled with being truthful and open in his marriage. He said that because of his pride and long habit of deceit, he often was not aware of his own motives and that his wife was frequently in the dark about what he was doing, feeling and thinking. I told him that while I understood the hurt he felt, he was going to have to start hating his deceit and dealing with it radically. His habit had been to be defensive and angry when confronted with his deceit. Such a reaction showed a lack of conviction, and only said to his wife that he was not facing his problem, that he never would overcome it. I advised him to become open and humble about his sin with those closest to him, and to invite them to speak up whenever they felt he was not being absolutely truthful. If he will do this, he can earn the trust and confidence of his wife and have a great, intimate marriage—but *only* when he becomes a man of truth!

Principles

A man of honor is a man of principle. A man of principle is faithful to what is right over and above his concern for his own safety, position or personal benefit. He stands up for what is right, no matter what the cost. It matters not to him which path is easier. He chooses what is right. It matters not what is popular: he does what God says. It does not matter if disapproval comes, even from those he loves the most: he is still unflinching. It matters not if his stand will transport him into a storm of conflict and disapproval: he does what is honorable. His is the attitude of Winston Churchill who said, as he lead Great Britain during World War 2, "into the storm, and through the storm."

Somewhere along the way, we will have opportunities to advance ourselves or keep ourselves out of trouble by going along with something wrong or by being silent in the face of injustice. Perhaps those doing the wrong are in a position to help or hurt us. Somewhere along the way, someone will expect out of us loyalty that leads to wrongdoing. They may want us to compromise sexually. They may want us to lie for them or to be silent as they lie. They may want us to leave them alone as they run over and abuse someone else. They may want us to be a part of their divisiveness and gossip. They may want us to join in their criticalness and complaining. "Aren't you loyal to me as a friend?" they will say. "Think about all I have done for you, all we have gone through together."

Some of the people we respect the most may sin and try to get us to go along in the name of loyalty. We must decide at those times if our loyalty is to God and to principle or to men. If you do not go along, they may try to get you to doubt yourself or blame you with being prideful. "Who do you think you are? What do you know?" will be their cry. You will have to decide that you know enough of God's word that you will not see it disobeyed by *anyone* without saying or doing something about it. If you get into trouble for that, then so be it. Better that than to be a man who stood by or participated in evil or unrighteous behavior. If someone will not listen to your appeal, it is their problem. But at least you have spoken up and can live before God with a clear conscience.

There have been times in my life when I was tempted but did not compromise. I look back to those moments with joy and with a righteous, solemn satisfaction. Those times were not easy, and in some cases I endured years of disapproval from someone I admired, but it was worth it in the end. These are the stands that define a man's life, that make or break his character, that make him a mighty man of God.

Daniel was a man who made such a decision. He and his friends were taken into exile by the Babylonians. He and several other of the most outstanding young men were given an opportunity to advance in the Persian government. They were to be trained in the wisdom of the nation and given positions of influence and trust. Instead of the lives of miserable slaves, they could become princely figures. Daniel did not turn down the opportunity, but he also would not compromise.

Daniel made a stand about the food he ate, resolving to abstain from the royal delicacies so that he might eat the foods

God had approved for his people. Not only did God protect Daniel as he upheld this conviction, but he also blessed him with exceptional intelligence and the ability to understand dreams and visions. King Nebuchadnezzar found Daniel and his friends who shared his convictions to be ten times wiser than the greatest magicians and wise men of Babylon.

Daniel realized that if he compromised even in one area, he would be heading down a road from which there was no return, where he could end up losing his faith and his relationship with God. God honored his stand with his blessing, and Daniel remained a man of integrity and honor throughout his life.

Sacrifice

The tests of honor are many, and Daniel would be tested many times. We find him later in life, having been awarded by King Nebuchadnezzar the governorship of the province of Babylon, with charge over all the king's wise men. His promotion arouses the envy of the other wise men, and they conceive a plot to overthrow him. They convince the new king, King Darius the Mede, to require that for the next thirty days no one in all the country should pray to any god but to the king himself, punishable by being cast into the lion's den. The king, who respected and loved Daniel, unthinkingly concurs, and the trap is set. It was Daniel's custom to pray to God in the open window of his home. Would he compromise? Would he hide away while praying to save his skin? Not this man of honor! The Bible records:

> Now when Daniel learned that the decree had been published, he went home to his upstairs room where the windows opened toward Jerusalem. Three times a day he got down on his knees and prayed, giving thanks to his God, just as he had done before. (Daniel 6:10)

Daniel's enemies seize the moment and report him to the king. In spite of his respect for Daniel, the king has to obey his own foolish decree, and Daniel is thrown into the lion's den. After a night of anguish, the king comes to see how he has fared. He finds Daniel alive and well! Daniel's reply to the king's inquiry as to his safety is:

"O king, live forever! My God sent his angel, and he shut the mouths of the lions. They have not hurt me, because I was found innocent in his sight. Nor have I ever done any wrong before you, O king." (Daniel 6:21-22)

We learn from these stories that honor and integrity are traits we must sacrifice for as young men, and they are qualities for which we must continue to pay the price all our lives. Sacrifice for the sake of honor will be richly rewarded by God. And, while God will not always deliver us *from* trouble, he will always deliver us when we are *in* trouble!

But sometimes loyalty to God and to principle means that we pay a price for which there is no immediate reward. It takes a man of great honor to step aside for someone else, to let himself fade into the background so another can do his work. Look at John the Baptist, the man of whom Jesus said, "Among those born of women there has not risen anyone greater than John the Baptist" (Matthew 11:11). He had a great ministry. He had faithful disciples. He was drawing crowds of thousands to the desert to hear him preach. But then, at immense personal cost, John stepped aside and allowed his cousin Jesus to supersede him, to take his place. His crowds and his disciples went over to Jesus. He told them that he was not the greatest but that another was greater than he: "After me will come one more powerful than I, the thongs of whose sandals I am not worthy to stoop down and untie" (Mark 1:7). John had lived to preach, to proclaim, to change lives. But then, he retired as a young man. His life shone only for a brief moment, and his work was done. He stands forever as the supreme example of a man who, out of honor for God and God's work, sacrifices his own way, his own feelings and his own career.

High Standards

A man of honor expects the best of himself. There is within mighty men a desire for excellence, a hunger to be the very best version of themselves that they can be. It is the drive of the divine within us, the impulse to leave behind our earthbound limitations and fulfill our true destiny—to be godly, and godlike. We are created in the image of God, and if we are disciples, we have the Spirit of God dwelling within us. We are therefore a mixture of the earthly and the divine, of heaven and earth, of flesh and spirit. A mighty man heeds the impulses of the image of God within him; he listens to the voice of the Spirit which within him continually calls out, "Go higher! Do more! Do better! Be better! Try harder! Give more! Do your best!" The man of honor does what love requires. He does what honors God and what he can present to God and man with legitimate pride of accomplishment.

The lesser man heeds another call: he only does enough to get by. He works until he is tired or bored or until his boss stops looking. He does enough to finish the job and say, "It is done," but not enough to finish and say, "It is well done!" He does what duty requires, but no more. The man without honor must continually be challenged, or he falls by the wayside. He must have supervision and prodding or he quits, or does a shoddy, half-done job.

Not so the man of honor. He does the best he can and is not at peace with himself if he knows he has done less. He appreciates the exhortations given him by others, but he does not rely upon them as his basis of motivation. He welcomes them as a way to raise his standards and as a way to do and be more, but not as a replacement for his own sense of righteous drive. He works whether he is supervised or not, because he does what he does for the glory of God. The passion to please and glorify God is so great within him that he rarely needs the prodding of others to urge him forward.

Who we are when we are alone is who we really are. It is then that our character manifests itself for good or ill. If we expect the best of ourselves, then we are men of honor, men of God, mighty men.

Challenge and Adventure

A man of honor embraces challenge and adventure. A man is made of flammable elements. There is something within his heart that is ignited by the sparks of challenge and adventure. It is God's desire to set him ablaze with the calling to a great cause, with the allure of great and mighty deeds to be done, or of glorious challenges to be braved and accomplished. The harder, the better. The more difficult, the more inspiring. The call for sacrifice only appeals to the best in his heart. The possibility of suffering and danger sets his blood boiling. The far-off prize only elicits a sparkling, steely gleam in his eye. Say it cannot be done, and now you have his attention! Say it is impossible, and he is on his knees, asking God for the strength to do that which on his own he cannot.

Let your manhood call you out of physical cowardice to climb a mountain, sail the sea or run a race. Let it call you out of laziness to the project, profession or deed that strikes fear in your bones. Let it summon you to take on the challenge whose prize will only be earned by blood, toil, tears and sweat. May it keep you going when you long to quit, but you know that honor—the honor of God and of your manhood—will not allow it.

All men have this spirit within them. It was put there by God. Some men let it burn, but others have quenched it through long years of failure to heed its voice. The call to glorious manhood is strong and great. Why do men thrill to the adventures of great military leaders and great sports heroes? Do not dismiss this impulse as the selfish craving for blood and violence. No, it is the soul of honor, the desire for greatness, the aspiration for the accomplishment of heroic deeds—placed in your heart by God. It is the rising of the best that is within you, not the worst. It is the clarion call to courage, to greatness, to true and noble manhood. It is this which is your salvation. It is this which will call you out of the twilight of mediocrity and dullness and into the sunshine of greatness. When you hear this call, heed it. Let its song of courage summon you to glory and beckon you to a better life, to be a man of honor, to be a mighty man of God! And if you do, at the end of your life, you will hear the words that every mighty man most longs to hear: "Well done, good and faithful servant, enter into the joys of your Lord!"

5

NOBILITY

He [is] an instrument for noble purposes, made holy, useful to the Master and prepared to do any good work.

2 Timothy 2:21

The man of nobility is a consummate gentleman. His noble stature is not given him as a privilege of birth; it is a hard-won attainment of character. He has a lofty air about him, a graciousness and distinction that is almost regal in its ethos. He is a man of kindness and sensitivity, who is also a man of courage, strength and principle. He melds the attributes of the warrior and shepherd in his life in an almost seamless combination that both impresses and moves those who know him. He combines qualities of character that almost seem contradictory—poise and passion, strength and gentleness, confidence and humility. Traits which most men possess in part, he has in whole.

This man makes us dream of a bygone era when men were chivalrous. He is the brave, unselfish knight whose quest is to befriend the forsaken, defend the weak and lift up the downtrodden. His compassionate strength warms our hearts and rekindles our hopes. Let us take a look at the character qualities of this man.

A Gentleman

A man of nobility is courteous and well-mannered. This is one of the great lessons that men need to learn. We should have learned manners from our parents, but many of them did not care to teach us. Others of us were taught, but we dismissed our lessons as a waste of time and as a concession to weakness and effeminacy. How wrong we were, and how much our manhood has suffered because of it! One of the great responsibilities we have as men is to be gentlemen and to train our sons to be gentlemen who carry themselves in a kind, courteous and lofty fashion.

Perhaps one way to understand the importance of being a gentleman is to see an example of someone who was not. We are told in the Bible the story of Nabal, a man who lived in the day of King David of Israel. For a time David lived in the Judean desert as a Robin Hood-type character, and he and his band of mighty men protected the farmers, shepherds and others who lived in the surrounding area. One day David sent some of his young men to the home of Nabal, hoping to receive some reward for the services that they had provided. But instead of receiving them with courtesy, Nabal rudely rebuffed them.

> *"Who is this David? Who is this son of Jesse? Many servants are breaking away from their masters these days. Why should I take my bread and water, and the meat I have slaughtered for my shearers, and give it to men coming from who knows where?" (1 Samuel 25:10-11)*

Sadly, many of us fancy ourselves as being strong and manly when we treat people this way. Instead, we only prove that we are selfish, discourteous and unkind men who are unworthy to be called gentlemen. We live in a world full of rude, mean people, and if we are not careful, we will become like them.

This story nearly ended tragically, with David taking vengeance on Nabal. Fortunately, Nabal's wife, Abigail, intervened and saved the day. God quickly took Nabal out of the picture, and upon his death David married Nabal's beautiful widow. God looks out for his gentlemen!

Kindness is evident in a man of nobility. He avoids embarrassing other people with sarcasm and harsh words. He is not rude or abrupt in his speech or tone of voice. He does not put other people down with words, expressions or deeds. He does not make others feel like they are an imposition upon his precious time or that he is too important to stop what he is doing to attend to their needs.

Courtesy is a hallmark of a noble man. He opens doors for others. He helps them carry their packages. He greets guests at the door and helps them with their coats. He brings a gift when he comes over for dinner. He picks up the dinner tab. When single men behave in these ways, young women want to be around them, go out with them and marry them! The appalling failure of young men to be courteous during courtship is one of the great reasons why fewer people are getting married today. Regardless of what some feminists say, women love to be treated with respect and deference, and I, for one, plan to keep on doing it.

One of the most gracious gentlemen I have known is Ignacio Garcia-Bengochea, the father of my friends, Carmen Garcia-Bentley and Elena Garcia-McKean. I have known Carmen and Elena's family since they were college students, and for many years our families lived in the same community. On one occasion, my wife, Geri, was on an airplane with two of our children. David and Elizabeth were very young at the time, and Geri was having difficulty managing them. Ignacio, who happened to be on the same flight for a business trip, noticed Geri's dilemma. He walked down the aisle and, smiling graciously, offered his assistance. He entertained three-year-old Elizabeth at his seat so that Geri could tend to our infant son. Geri was deeply appreciative and has never forgotten his kindness, even after the passing of many years. Ignacio, a true gentleman, saw a lady in distress and dropped what he was doing to help her. This is what nobility of spirit is all about.

Unselfish

A man of nobility puts himself last; he is unselfish. He thinks of others before he thinks of himself. The unselfish man is a thoughtful servant. To be in his presence is to have his mind and attention fixed upon you. He is always looking for ways to serve, to show respect and to make you feel honored and important. To be in his home is to be treated as if you were royalty. You are made to feel entirely welcome. Your every need is tended to. It would be a terrible embarrassment to this man for you to feel uncomfortable or not warmly received by him and his family.

Such a man is Bob Shaheen. I met Bob and his wife Patricia when they lived in New York City. They eventually moved to Miami and were there during the closing months of our time there. In discussing this chapter, I asked Geri who were the gentlemen she had known that most impressed her. Her eyes brightened, and she immediately mentioned Bob. "You just feel better being around him," she said. "He is so gracious and kind that he makes you feel better about yourself." Bob always makes you feel as if you are the most important person in his world. He drops whatever he is doing to warmly greet you. He never makes you feel as if you're putting him out in any way. Bob's technique in taking you to dinner is to speak privately to the maitre d' ahead of time and arrange for the bill to be discreetly brought to him. In this way, you never have a chance to have an argument—the bill has been paid before there is ever any discussion.

To be around some men, however, is to be made to feel that you are a bother. Their rudeness, abruptness and surly demeanor make you feel uncomfortable and ill at ease. Such men are selfish. They are consumed with their own thoughts and concerns. They do not have time to see above their petty problems and act as gentlemen. Such men offend others. Especially do they hurt the feelings of their wives. Some husbands are so discourteous that their wives fear having guests over to visit. These men assume a sullen air of distance and unhappiness at family gatherings: they retreat to a corner or to the television, or worse yet, absent themselves from the house altogether. How rude, how unkind, how ignoble!

Gracious

A man of nobility is a gracious man. The Bible teaches us that God is "slow to anger" and that "he does not treat us as our sins deserve" (Psalm 103:8, 10). A gracious man gives you the mercy you need rather than the justice you deserve. He holds you to high standards but is not petty and legalistic in the way he does so.

Some men are so austere and stern that the people around them continually live in fear of offending them. Everyone walks on eggshells around such men. If you make a mistake, you will receive swift, severe and merciless retribution. This attitude only makes people more ill at ease and more likely to make mistakes! Most of all, this attitude makes people miserable. No one enjoys working for someone like this, being in a family like this or, God forbid, being in a church like this.

Think about all the mistakes made by Jesus' apostles. They certainly felt free to make them! They had no hesitation in approaching Jesus and even asked to sit at his right and left side (Mark 10:35-37). They openly expressed their opinions. Peter even disagreed with Jesus. He was wrong, and he was strongly corrected, but it shows that Jesus created an atmosphere of openness. The only other time Jesus severely reprimanded the disciples was when they were oppressive in their attitudes toward children (Mark 10:13-16).

How about you? Are you gracious and easygoing, or do you make everything a federal case? Do the people around you constantly feel that they live with displeasure and disapproval? Are they afraid that if they make the smallest mistake, you will become sullen and angry—and that you will harshly reprimand them? If so, you need to see how you are harming those nearest you and immediately take steps to change.

Rational

A man of nobility is a reasonable and approachable man. A Christian gentleman is a man who can be talked to. You can go to a man like this, ask for an audience and receive it quickly, graciously and without fanfare. He is a man who can be reasoned with. He is someone with whom you can sit down and pour out your heart and mind, knowing that you will be heard. He listens, and listens carefully. He does not jump to conclusions and close down communication. Instead, he knows that it is often difficult for people to say what is on their minds, and he asks many questions before he gives a reply. He withholds judgment until he has all the facts. He changes his mind when presented with new information or with a compelling argument. Above all, he is fair and just. He does not formulate his judgments based upon personal preference and prejudice, but upon that which is true and righteous. He does not allow his own mood, state of mind or physical weariness to keep him from thinking clearly.

You leave his presence feeling that you have been completely heard and understood. Then, even if he gives counsel that is contrary to what you wanted to hear, you still know that you have been fairly treated and are thus much more likely to respect and heed the advice that he gave.

The man who thinks he must quickly render an opinion on everything to prove his wisdom and strength is only making himself a fool. The man who has certain things in his life about which he is extremely prejudiced disqualifies himself as a respected and judicious leader. He will alienate and estrange himself from his closest friends and coworkers. He will also exasperate and frustrate his wife and children. Those around him never feel that they are given fair treatment, but instead they feel prejudged and marginalized. The sullen, angry looks and discouraged and beaten down appearances of this man's inner circle betray that he is not a man of noble judgment.

I would urge you to develop the quality of gentleness. The Greek scholars translate this word as "sweet reasonableness." Paul said in Philippians 4:4-5, "Rejoice in the Lord always. I will say it again: Rejoice! Let your gentleness be evident to all. The Lord is near." Be the kind of man who will listen with attentiveness, sensitivity and heart. Hear the facts, but see beyond the facts to the feelings and emotions behind them. Then, even when you have to take an unpopular stand, you can do so knowing that everyone has had a fair hearing.

We must learn to discern between matters of principle and personal preference. Issues of conviction and principle are worth making a stand for, but matters of opinion usually are not. Opinions do matter, but we must carefully decide when they are so important that we must not compromise. Matters that have to do with sin, righteousness and with the basics of the gospel message are worth standing up for, but issues concerning our personal feelings, roles or opinions are not as vital. Oftentimes our problem is that we give way in areas of principle and are stubborn in areas of opinion. The man of nobility knows the difference between the two and lives his life accordingly.

Above Pettiness

A man of nobility is above pettiness. We have already seen how Jesus laid aside his rights for the sake of others. We have just discussed the importance of learning what is vital and what is not. A man who is petty is forever making mountains out of molehills. He is forever getting worked up over the wrong things. What am I talking about?

The petty man is easily slighted. And since he is self-centered, he often feels slighted! If he feels he is not accorded proper respect, he becomes sullen. This man is forever in a state of dissatisfaction and unhappiness. If he feels in the least slighted or ignored, he angrily withdraws. He easily becomes critical. How many an occasion, how many an evening, has been ruined for the wife of a man like this! She is continually worrying about how he feels and his perceptions about how he is being treated. She either becomes a diplomat, forever trying to get him to the peace table with everyone or begins to share in his feeling that he is continually being mistreated.

Are not many of our feelings of rejection brought on because we are at the same time so proud and so low in self-esteem? Is it not because there is one part of us that craves to be exalted and another that feels inferior? To overcome this terrible flaw, we must become men who are so centered in God's evaluation of us that what others think (or what we imagine they think!) cannot destroy our poise and equilibrium.

Sometimes we will be treated wrongly. What then? How are we to react? Here is how: *We should be above it.* We should not let it get under our skin. We should rise above mistreatment and be men of true nobility of spirit. Jesus was quite often treated disrespectfully. It did not faze him. He became offended only when God's name and reputation were on the line, or when the rights of the weak and poor were being trampled. Jesus' face could be slapped, he could be spat upon, and his name be cursed, but he would not react. It was because he was not a petty man.

Similarly, a man of nobility is above trivial arguments. He does not foolishly quarrel. Paul told Timothy that "the Lord's servant must not quarrel" (2 Timothy 2:24). Arguing and bickering are beneath the mighty man of God. He simply will not allow himself to be drawn into foolish contentions. Most of what we quarrel over is not worth it. The man of nobility, like Jesus, focuses on the heart of the matter and is not distracted by extraneous issues.

Above Vulgarity

The man of nobility is above vulgarity. The noble man has an attitude of reverence—reverence for God, reverence for life and reverence for people. He does not drag down into the gutter those things which should be regarded as holy and noble.

He has a holy outlook on sexual matters. He does not speak openly of that which should be discussed only in private. He does not trivialize and defile sex by coarse and crass jokes. He does not tear down women by calling them degrading and dirty names.

The world we live in is becoming increasingly vulgar. Movies, television—you name it—all are going deeper into the gutter. It seems we have no shame anymore. People will talk about anything on television and use the worst kind of language in any situation. We have lost our reverence for life. Not so the mighty man of God! The Bible says "be holy, because I am holy" (Leviticus 11:44). This man has a lofty view of everything that God made; he will not be defiled by the way he speaks or acts.

A man of nobility will not engage in boorish behavior in any setting, whether in public or in his own home. He is well-mannered. He politely waits to eat until all have been served. He does not reach across the table, grabbing for the food like a barbarian. He avoids locker room talk and behavior, especially in the presence of women and children. He does not tell the kinds of stories that humiliate and embarrass his wife, his friends or the people around him—he is simply above it. The noble man is a living embodiment of all that is gracious, lofty and decent in manhood.

The call to nobility is a challenge for men of God to rise up and become gentlemen. It is a call for us to leave behind the brutish and boorish ways of the world and become men of manners, civility and decency. It is a summons for us to become men of true strength, men who do not have to run over other people to prove our manhood. It is an appeal for us to be men who lay aside our own opinions so that we might stand up for the principles of God. It is a challenge for us to forsake discourtesy and selfishness, to become chivalrous knights who look out for ourselves last and the needs of others first. It is a call for us to rise up and stand out as men of graciousness, refinement and honor.

I pray that the men reading these words will take them to heart and make radical changes. Your wives, your children, your coworkers and your friends will notice the difference. And when they do, they will freely give you their admiration, respect and devotion.

6

PURITY

Keep yourself pure.

1 Timothy 5:22

Remaining sexually pure is one of the greatest challenges in a man's life. To refrain from sexual relations while single and to remain faithful to your wife "until death separates you" is one of your most sacred commitments.

To unspiritual men, this may seem foolish, but not to a mighty man of God. A mighty man values God's approval so highly that he seeks it above all else. This man respects women and does not regard them as objects of his personal gratification. A righteous man of God respects his girlfriend or fiancée and will never take advantage of her trust. A true man of God values his marriage and would do nothing to damage it. A godly man values the respect and happiness of his children and desires to never do anything to shame them or to shame their mother. He remembers that there are those who look up to him, who count on him to be righteous. A man of purity values his mind and will not allow it to be defiled by thinking lustful thoughts; and he values his eyes and will not allow them to gaze upon that which is forbidden or which belongs to another. A mighty man of God reveres and respects his own body and will not degrade it by engaging in sexual immorality.

Joseph: Hero of Purity

The great hero of sexual purity in the Bible is Joseph, the son of Jacob. When he was only a teenager, Joseph was sold into slavery by his jealous brothers. He was purchased by an Egyptian named Potiphar, the captain of Pharaoh's bodyguard. By virtue of his diligence and hard work, Joseph earned Potiphar's trust and rose to a position of great responsibility in his household. Joseph was a handsome young man, and he caught the eye of Potiphar's wife. This unscrupulous woman decided that Joseph would be an easy mark for her. She propositioned Joseph, but he turned her down. She continued her advances for many days, but the answer from this noble young man was "How then could I do such a wicked thing and sin against God?" (Genesis 39:9). He tried to avoid her, but she kept on pursuing him. Finally, she physically groped him, insisting that he give in. Joseph ran out the door, leaving the rejected woman holding his robe.

In anger and pride, Potiphar's wife took vengeance. Brandishing Joseph's robe, she told her husband that Joseph had tried to seduce her but that she fended him off. The result was a jail sentence for Joseph. If you know the rest of the story, you know that Joseph did not become bitter. As a matter of fact, he rose to the top again—this time to be placed in charge of the prison. Finally, in an amazing turnaround, Joseph was freed by Pharaoh who appointed him the second-highest official in the nation of Egypt!

How many of us would have been strong, like Joseph? How many of us would have resisted the temptation of an easy sexual exploit? Joseph was a young man, far away from his own family and from the godly teachings he had learned as a boy. He might have reasoned that a sexual compromise would do him no harm. She was a wealthy, influential woman; he was under her authority; it would be to his advantage to please her, to give in. She was the wife of a high official and was probably an attractive, desirable woman.

Let us be men of strength and conviction like Joseph. Let us not define our manhood according to the standards of the world, but by the standards of God's word. God's way is best; God's way is right. Be a man of purity!

Deception of Sin

One of the best ways to conquer sexual impurity is by seeing its futility. No sin promises more and delivers less than sexual immorality. It pledges excitement and pleasure, but gives us misery and emptiness. It promises to fulfill our manhood, but destroys it instead. It appeals to our pride, but covers us with shame. In the end, we hang our heads in defeat and agony, asking ourselves, *Why? Why was I such a fool?* And after the moment is over, we have a lifetime to remember and regret our folly.

We throw away our honor when we give up our virginity. No longer can we say to the woman we marry, "I have saved myself for you and you alone." Now we have opened the door to further temptation, to greater sin. When we are sexually immoral with the woman we plan to marry, we have dishonored and forever stained our relationship. We have lost the mutual respect that comes from purity. If you do later marry each other, you will have to struggle to regain respect for one another, and you will battle to experience fulfilling intimacy.

When we commit adultery, we violate our promise to the woman we love. We break the most sacred pledge a man can make, aside from our pledge to God himself. We take that which we promised to preserve for our wife alone and give it to another. We take the most intimate and defining act of our marriage and share it with someone to whom it does not belong. We dishonor ourselves; we dishonor our wives. We lose their trust. If we try to hide our sin, we will live with haunting, gnawing guilt and with the icy fear of discovery. Every time we make love to our wives, the memory of our adultery will hover between us like a silent, unseen veil, separating us and robbing us of the pleasure of married love. Our wives will sense it, and they will find us out!

If you have children, your shame is multiplied. You have sinned against them by sinning against their mother. You have harmed the woman who gave them birth. They hold your union sacred and want you to be faithful to one another. They will lose respect for you, even come to resent and hate you. They will be likely to imitate your sin. Imagine your sons sinning in this way in their marriages—is this what you want for them? Imagine your daughter having to bear the sorrow of her husband's adultery—imagine her heartache, her shame, her pain. Face what your actions will do to your wife and your children. No moment of pleasure, no other woman is worth it. You will destroy everything you hold dear. Think about it, and stop before you make the mistake of a lifetime!

Avoiding Impurity

To avoid sexual sin, steer clear of weakening circumstances and tempting women. If you are dating, avoid any situations of isolation where sexual passion could overcome you. If you are a married man and are seriously attracted to another woman, avoid her. Do whatever it takes. If it means getting a transfer to another workplace, do it. If it means quitting your job, then quit. Be willing to take radical steps.

> *"Woe to the world because of the things that cause people to sin! Such things must come, but woe to the man through whom they come! If your hand or your foot causes you to sin, cut it off and throw it away. It is better for you to enter life maimed or crippled than to have two hands or two feet and be thrown into eternal fire. And if your eye causes you to sin, gouge it out and throw it away. It is better for you to enter life with one eye than to have two eyes and be thrown into the fire of hell."* (Matthew 18:7-9)

Be open about your temptations. One of the great ways to take the allure out of sexual temptation is by exposing it to righteous men. Have other men in your life hold you accountable. It is wise for those of us who are married to share our sexual temptations with other married men because, as men, they understand the nature of male sexual desire. There is a time to tell our wives of our temptations, but to do so too frequently or as a first line of defense is unwise. This may subject our wives to unnecessary struggles with anger and resentment and can undermine their confidence as well. Before making that kind of disclosure, it is best to seek wise advice. (The same is true, and even more crucial, if you have already been involved in adultery. Before any discussion with your wife, I would urge you to consult experienced spiritual advisors.)

A High Standard

Jesus in his teachings raises the standards of sexual behavior to a new level. Not only is the act of adultery wrong, but so is illicit sexual desire:

> "You have heard that it was said, 'Do not commit adultery.' But I tell you that anyone who looks at a woman lustfully has already committed adultery with her in his heart." (Matthew 5:27-28)

Jesus wants sexual sin to be dealt with at the root. He says we must deal with our sinful desires. Some would say that this is an impossible or unrealistic expectation that no normal man can attain. Let us carefully examine Jesus' command and see just how wise and effective a teaching it is.

Defining Lust

Jesus declares that looking at a woman lustfully is sinful. But what exactly is lust? How do we know when we have crossed the line from innocent attraction to sinful lust? We must learn to identify exactly what lust is so that we can pick the right battles to fight.

Perhaps the best place to start is to say what lust is *not.* We have not lusted just because we notice that a woman is beautiful or attractive. To be aware of a woman's appearance is a natural part of manhood and is not wrong. There is no innate harm in noticing feminine beauty that does not present itself in a provocative manner. To attempt to avoid seeing women or to fail to acknowledge that they are attractive is impossible and unnatural. This is what some of the medieval monks tried to do, and it is not too difficult to see that this is not what Jesus meant by his teaching or practiced in his own life.

What then is lust? How do we define it? Lust is desire. Lust occurs when innocent attraction escalates to the level of craving and arousal. It is looking at a woman with the *intent* to desire her. The crucial question is, then, with what intent are you looking? If you are looking in order to lust, you are sinning. If you are looking because a woman is behaving in a sensual manner or is seductively dressed, you are lusting. This would include looking at sexually provocative printed materials, videos or movies. It would include reading about sexual activity or talking about it (phone sex, flirtation, etc.). It would include viewing Internet pornography and involvement in sexually oriented Internet chat rooms. It would include using your imagination to fantasize sexual activities or sexual images.

But lust is not just a matter of intent, it is a matter of *degree*. Our blameless noticing can escalate to sinful desire. This can happen even though our original intentions were pure, and this is why lust is so challenging for us. We must be on our guard that we do not allow even the most innocent of circumstances to lead us into sin.

So, then, when does harmless attraction end and lust begin? It happens when we allow our thoughts and eyes to wander where they should not, when we do not stop our feelings before they turn to sin. Sometimes this can happen rather quickly, especially if a woman is improperly or seductively clothed, or if she behaves in a flirtatious manner (whether perceived or real). There is then a line we cross when the innocent noticing of beauty turns to lust. I cannot give you a precise definition of when we cross that line, but just between us guys, most of us know when we are approaching it! And it is better to stay far from it than to see how close we can get without sinning!

Some men lack a tender conscience about lust, and other men are plagued with overactive consciences that condemn them with unnecessary guilt. The former need conviction; the latter need education. If you are in the first group, I would urge you to gain conviction before you ruin your life; if you are in the latter category, and especially if you are young or are new to the faith, I would urge consultation with spiritual, mature men who can help you navigate your way through these treacherous waters.

Overcoming Lust

Now that we have defined lust, let us focus our attention upon how we may overcome it. Let me offer some practical advice.

Don't let it start. This is the best way to stop lust. Quickly turn away when your eyes begin to lead you into sin. Do not let yourself remain in a situation that will entice you to become aroused. The quicker you deal with lust, the less of a chance it has to take root. It is amazing how weak and pathetic lust appears when you stay far from it. The less it is indulged, the more it is exposed for its foolishness and emptiness.

Do not watch movies alone. Attend movies with others of like convictions. When you view a video, do so only with others present. Watching television in isolation is a bad idea, even when the program seems harmless. The program can change, the advertisements are often suggestive, and there is always the temptation to search for a provocative program. This is especially true of late-night viewing.

Create roadblocks. Set up blockages that deny lust a foothold. For example, if you have home access to the Internet, you may need to install a program that blocks access to pornographic Web sites. (You also may need to avoid other Web sites that have that kind of access.) If you are going out of town and will be exposed to increased temptation, set up a phone calling schedule with your wife or a male friend. Don't go out with friends or fellow employees unless you know that the atmosphere will be wholesome. If the atmosphere becomes suggestive, immediately excuse yourself.

Be open about your temptations. Temptation flourishes in secret and in the darkness. In these situations, its allure seems irresistible. But when we expose it to the light, to the knowledge of righteous friends, its power is broken.

If you have succumbed to lust, do not hide it or put off confessing it. The longer you hold in your sin, the greater the opportunity to repeat it. The longer you delay, the more guilt and discouragement you will feel. One of the great tools Satan will use against us when we lust is that of discouragement. He will tell us that we cannot change, or he will make us think we are the only one who struggles in this way. Sometimes, even when we have privately confessed to God, we are not sure if we have genuinely repented. At other times, we may not be sure how serious a violation we have committed. It is impossible for us to figure all of this out on our own! We must be open, and we must get help. The longer we wait, the longer we are exposed to danger.

See lust in all of its folly. Lust gives us nothing! It dangles before our eyes that which is not ours. When we lust, we long for that which we can never truly possess. We are playing Satan's game, and he always wins. He laughs at us for the fools we are. The women we lust after in the movies and in pornography will never be ours. It is a big tease, with nothing but emptiness and frustration at the end.

Men who allow themselves to view these sights and engage in masturbation are the biggest fools of all. Masturbation is a road to slavery, selfishness and weirdness. It can never satisfy and can never give the fulfillment that married love provides. It is a sin against God and is the prison of the tormented, the weak and the lonely.

Homosexuality

The Bible speaks in no uncertain terms about sexual involvement with other men.

> *"Because of this, God gave them over to shameful lusts. Even their women exchanged natural relations for unnatural ones. In the same way the men also abandoned natural relations with women and were inflamed with lust for one another. Men committed indecent acts with other men, and received in themselves the due penalty for their perversion." (Romans 1:26-27)*

> *"Do you not know that the wicked will not inherit the kingdom of God? Do not be deceived: Neither the sexually immoral nor idolaters nor adulterers nor male prostitutes nor homosexual offenders nor thieves nor the greedy nor drunkards nor slanderers nor swindlers will inherit the kingdom of God. (1 Corinthians 6:9-10)*

> *"Do not lie with a man as one lies with a woman; that is detestable." (Leviticus 18:22)*

These scriptures, along with many others, make it clear that homosexual activity and homosexual lust are sinful. They are clearly condemned by God. In spite of what we read in the popular press, in spite of the talk shows, in spite of the claims of misguided religionists, in spite of the distortions of some who claim a genetic justification, homosexuality is wrong. It is dead wrong. There is no room for doubt, and no room for debate on this issue. The Bible could not be clearer than it is.

Not only is homosexuality sinful, it is an abandonment of the natural order (Romans 1:26, 27). While it is true that some men may be more disposed to this temptation than others, there is no basis for the claim that some of us are naturally this way. God does not create homosexuals, nor is anyone born that way. Homosexuality is a sinful, learned behavior.

Homosexual desire is a warping of natural sexual desire for women into sexual desire for men. The desires are real, and thus may seem "natural" to the one who experiences them, but they are not an inherent part of a man's nature and are instead a denial of his true masculinity. Nothing is quite as destructive to male personality as homosexuality. In years of working with men afflicted with this problem, I have never met a man involved in it who was happy. Perhaps one of the greatest ironies of all is the corruption of the word "gay" to describe the homosexual lifestyle.

My observation is that many of them were lured into homosexuality by the influence of another male, usually someone older. Others were drawn into homosexuality by an unfortunate sexual experience in their childhood or by damaging factors in their family lives. Such men may think they are inherently homosexual, but they are mistaken. They have learned the behavior and the attraction. They may have learned it at a very young age, but learn it they did.

The good news is that homosexuality can be repented of, forgiven and overcome. In my nearly thirty years in the ministry, I have seen many men overcome this sin. It is not a transgression that leaves one beyond the reach of the grace of God. It is not an offense that ostracizes one from the loving outreach of the church or that leaves one in a state where redemption and rebuilding are impossible. Homosexuality can be forgiven, and homosexuals can become masculine, manly men. Many homosexuals can be restored to a complete heterosexual attraction and can become happily married men with families. Others can be freed from a predominate homosexual attraction and will find that the desire for men diminishes the longer they remain on a righteous path. Although it is painful and difficult, married men who get involved in homosexual sin can have their marriages restored. This is not to say that homosexuality is easy to overcome or that these men never again have to face temptation, but it is to say that they are able to leave their past behind and build new lives.

A man who has had a homosexual past will need much encouragement and wise counsel. He will also need strong, masculine men as his friends. Some former homosexuals can and should marry; perhaps others should not. But the great news is that just as the early church converted and helped men of this background, so can we today. There are many men in God's kingdom today who are overcoming this sin and who now have great male friendships that are wholesome and righteous. If a man wants to change, and is willing to trust in God, the power of God is available to him and amazing transformation can occur!

Becoming a Man of Purity

If reading this chapter has exposed unconfessed sexual sin in your life, deal with it today. Be open about your sin with those who can help you to overcome it, according to the teachings of God's word. If you have sexually compromised yourself in the past and have repented, leave it there. Do not let the words of this chapter reopen old wounds, but rather strengthen your resolve to remain pure for the rest of your life. Let us go to God for forgiveness, cleansing and the power to change. Let us be born again to a new life and a new hope. Let us resolve to be different in the future!

If you are single, overcome evil with good. Use your single lifestyle as a greater opportunity to serve God and his kingdom more fervently. Devote yourself to growing spiritually, so that you will one day be ready for the great commitment of marriage if that is God's will for you. When you are tempted with discouragement, remember the great blessings of married life that await you, and be patient.

If you are married, find sexual fulfillment in your marriage. The joys and pleasure of romantic love in marriage are one of God's greatest blessings. Life is not meant to be one long battle with sexual lust. Instead, we are meant to be pure, to resist temptation and to live sexually satisfied lives as married men. We should be more preoccupied with our love and attraction for our wives than the evils of temptation.

We will close our thoughts with these words from the book of Proverbs, which give us not only a warning against sexual sin, but reveal to us the glorious joys of married life:

> *Drink water from your own cistern,*
> *running water from your own well.*
> *Should your springs overflow in the streets,*
> *your streams of water in the public squares?*
> *Let them be yours alone,*
> *never to be shared with strangers.*
> *May your fountain be blessed,*
> *and may you rejoice in the wife of your youth.*
> *A loving doe, a graceful deer—*
> *may her breasts satisfy you always,*
> *may you ever be captivated by her love.*
> *Why be captivated, my son, by an adulteress?*
> *Why embrace the bosom of another man's wife?*
> *(Proverbs 5:15-20)*

7

Lovingkindness

When the Lord saw her, his heart went out to her and he said, "Don't cry."

Luke 7:13

Do you have a tender heart? Is your heart moved by the feelings and sufferings of others? Are you filled with compassion for those who are hurting? The mighty man has a kind, loving heart. He has a soul that feels and cares. He is sensitive to suffering and pain. The heart of a mighty man hurts for those in emotional and spiritual distress. He feels what they feel, and because he loves others as he loves himself, he cares and reaches out to help them. In his strength the man of God never neglects or takes advantage of the weak, but instead devotes himself to lifting them up. His power and influence with others flows from his heart of lovingkindness.

Compassion

The heart of Jesus was a heart that went out in full measure to those in need. Whatever the pain and whoever suffered it, Jesus' compassion went forth to them. Isn't this the secret of his greatness? Isn't this why he is the greatest man the world has ever known? It is Jesus' great heart of lovingkindness that wins our devotion. Isn't this why you follow him, because he cares about you? It is why I have stayed with him for thirty years and will remain with him until I die. Nothing draws us to Jesus more than his tender, sensitive and noble heart of love.

I am weary of men who hide behind their manliness as an excuse for insensitivity. I am offended and angered by men who claim to know Jesus, but are very distant from his heart of tenderness and compassion. Such men may justify themselves in the name of strength and conviction, but it is really only an excuse for a hard, harsh, uncaring and selfish soul. I am sick of seeing it. I am sick of hearing it. Such a masquerade of manhood must cease!

Respect for Women

Observe Jesus' treatment of women. He came into a world that regarded women as drudges or toys and lifted them to the heights of respect and reverence. He scandalized his name and hastened his crucifixion by so doing, but he gladly paid the price for his chivalry. Is there any example of him speaking unkindly to a woman? Even when he had to chide his mother, he did so with gentleness and respect. He was kind to widows and rebuked those who neglected them. He commended the poor widow who gave all she had to the temple treasury and brought back to life the son of another grieving widow. His heart even went out in sympathy to the women of the street, the prostitutes. While others looked upon them with disgust and embarrassment, Jesus reached out and touched them. He said that such women would get into the kingdom of God before the religious people of his day.

He shamed the self-righteous, hypocritical men who held one standard for themselves and another for women with his unforgettable words: "If any one of you is without sin, let him be the first to throw a stone at her" (John 8:7). He took the time to speak to an outcast Samaritan woman who had had five husbands and was at that time with a live-in lover, because he saw in her a thirst for what was right and noble. From that conversation a village and a nation were saved. While in agony on the cross, he looked down with eyes of compassion, saw his grieving mother and sent her to live for the rest of her days with the beloved apostle John. Jesus is the greatest defender of womanhood the world has ever known.

The mighty man of God imitates Jesus in his respect and consideration of women. A true man never takes advantage of his position of physical strength or leadership to mistreat a woman in any way. I have seen brothers in the church who are fearful in rebuking other men but brave in correcting the sisters. I suggest that such men are just plain cowards. There are others who will exonerate the men and blame the women in just about any dispute or counseling situation. Such men are harsh and twisted in their judgment and could use a lesson in compassion from him who was called "Wonderful Counselor" (Isaiah 9:6).

Consideration means that we listen when women talk. It means that when they are right, we willingly concede the point. Some men feel that to prove themselves, they need to dominate and control conversation. They feel that to seek a woman's wisdom would be a sign of weakness and would bring disrespect upon themselves. Such men do not take a woman's opinion seriously. They dismiss women as being spiritual and intellectual lightweights. For these men to yield their opinions to women or to admit to them that they are wrong would be, in their minds, a crippling blow to their masculinity.

I learned long ago to listen to the women in my life and to seek their advice. The wise, intuitive insight I have received has saved me from many a mistake and guided me to victory countless times. Women often have insight that men lack, and we are fools not to give ear to them. My wife, Geri, is my wisest counselor and best critic. No one has helped me more to be the man that God would have me to be. She complements me perfectly. We constantly exchange our views with one another. In our family life and in serving side by side in the ministry, I would not dream of moving forward on matters great or small without seeking her wisdom. She is a gold mine of ideas. Her conceptions are creative, insightful, forward-thinking, on-target and are greatly responsible for our family's happiness and for much of the success that the Triangle Church has enjoyed.

Love for Children

The mighty man imitates Jesus in his attitude of loving-kindness toward children. Jesus cared about children and admired their innocence and purity. When his disciples rebuked the crowds for bringing children to him, Jesus became indignant. It was one of the few times Jesus became angry, and it was because the rights and needs of children were being trampled. If you think you are too important or too busy for children, you are not a Christlike man and have disqualified yourself from being a mighty man of God. Take the time to learn how to comfort, play with and patiently teach a child. Afterward, you will feel like it is you who have learned as much as or more than they have!

You can tell a great deal about men by the demeanor of the women and children in their lives. If the women around them are radiantly happy and secure, those men have hearts of lovingkindness. If their children are smiling and assured, if they look you confidently in the eye as they speak to you, then their fathers are loving men. If, on the other hand, the children are sullen and walk beneath a cloud of gloom, worry and fear, in all likelihood there is something deeply wrong with the men in their lives. Such men are not mighty men and are not worthy heroes for their families or for our churches.

The Example of Jesus

Though Jesus was a man of granitic conviction and righteousness, somehow people felt that they could approach him. They felt free to ask him for relief from their sufferings. They had no hesitation in touching him as he strode through the crowds. They felt that they could ask him questions. Even his enemies felt free to speak to him. Simply put, Jesus was a warm, affectionate and approachable man.

Our goal as mighty men must be to imitate Jesus in his lovingkindness. Some of us will have to redefine our understanding of manhood. We will have to learn to detest our harsh behaviors just as Jesus does. It will mean admitting that we have been wrong and being willing to do whatever it takes to change. For others of us, these thoughts may come as a welcome relief. We have had feelings of compassion in our hearts, but have wondered if they were signs of weakness. I have good news—they were not signs of weakness, but the promptings of the Holy Spirit! We need to stop quenching the Spirit and let our feelings of warmth and tenderness flow unhindered, letting them lead us to feel and act in the way Jesus did, with a heart of lovingkindness.

I remember the difficulty I had as I began to try to become an expressive, loving person. It was like learning a new language. I felt clumsy and awkward. I embarrassed myself as I tried to reach out. I often wondered if others considered me a fool or questioned my motives. I sometimes still do. But I resolved that looking or feeling foolish was a small price to pay for the benefit of learning how to love. I concluded that the biggest fool of all was the man who, for fear of embarrassing himself, failed to express his love to those he cared for. I started working on being more affectionate. I remember coming home from college one weekend and giving my mom a big hug. She almost fainted. Now she expects it! I started saying "I love you" much more, and then going further and telling people why I love them. I began to write cards in which I did more than offer a perfunctory greeting; instead, I poured out my love, gratitude, appreciation and respect. I started to let myself cry as I tried to tell people how much I cared.

I wouldn't go back to being my old self for the world! I no longer care if people wonder what has gotten into me. I just want them to know I love them. I would rather be considered an expressive fool than to look back one day regretting that I failed to tell my loved ones how deeply I cared for them.

Learn to feel. Learn to care. Take people into your heart. Become a man who refreshes others with lovingkindness. When you do, the people around you will blossom. They will bloom with a newfound joy, they will grow, they will change, they will be full of life. Their long-dormant talent, their hidden greatness, will flower in the sunshine of your love.

Give your love. Give it freely; give it without regard to your pride. Hold nothing back. Love freely, love warmly, love kindly, love as you have never dared to love before. Then one day, long after you are gone, you will be remembered with the greatest compliment you could ever receive: "He was a man who loved."

8

JOY

So I commend the enjoyment of life, because nothing is better for a man under the sun than to eat and drink and be glad. Then joy will accompany him in his work all the days of the life God has given him under the sun.

Ecclesiastes 8:15

Joy! I love the sound of the word, even the way it looks on a page: Joy! The second fruit of the Spirit, the overwhelming sentiment of heaven, the watchword of the early church, the heart and soul of the gospel: "I bring you good news of great joy that will be for all the people" (Luke 2:10).

A Celebration

When God touches a human life, it blossoms with song and happiness. After the Israelites crossed the Red Sea, they broke out the tambourines and sang a song of thundering, joyful praise. When David brought the ark into Jerusalem, he danced with all his might. When Ezra and Nehemiah restored the temple, they banned sadness and crying, saying "Do not grieve, for the joy of the Lord is your strength" (Nehemiah 8:10). When Isaiah looked forward to the coming of the new covenant, he described the life of God's children in these exultant words:

> *You will go out in joy*
> *and be led forth in peace;*
> *the mountains and hills*
> *will burst into song before you,*

> and all the trees of the field
>   will clap their hands.
> Instead of the thornbush will grow the
>   pine tree,
>   and instead of briers the myrtle will grow.
> This will be for the LORD's renown,
>   for an everlasting sign,
>   which will not be destroyed." (Isaiah 55:12-13)

Joy flowed around the life and ministry of Jesus, gloriously fulfilling the promise of these words. The crowds around him celebrated, tearing off their coats and laying them under his feet. They scaled trees to see him, brought down the branches to give him a worthy pathway and cried out his praise. The Pharisees said they should stop, but Jesus replied that if they were silent, the rocks would break out in song! When Jesus entered the temple, the children shouted in jubilation, once again dismaying the Pharisees. But Jesus simply refused to deny the kingdom the playful, uninhibited celebration of life. So great was the joy around Jesus that people ran up to him begging to join his movement. He had to let them know that in spite of all the abounding cheerfulness they saw, his way was one of self- denial and difficulty and that at night he had no place to lay his head. Jesus was criticized for being too joyful. He was accused of being a glutton and a drunkard. He was not, but one thing we know: he found the joy of life that gluttons and drunkards seek in misguided ways.

When Jesus was seen alive again after his crucifixion, the disciples were so happy that they did not believe it for joy—it was too good to be true. But it was and is true! Gloriously, beautifully, rapturously, beyond-our-wildest-dreams true! Our sins are forgiven. We have the Holy Spirit within us to ensure our place in heaven and to comfort and empower us until we get there. We have the church, the glorious bride of Christ, the City Set on a Hill, as our family and dwelling place while we remain on this earth. And we have the Bible to guide us and prayer to sustain us. We, above all people, should be overflowing with joy!

Men in God's kingdom should lead the way in the celebration. We should be mighty men of joy! We should not be following along in the dust behind the women and children, cautioning them to not let things get out of hand—no, we should be in the front of the procession, leading the way in the joyful praises of God. Let us not imitate the older brother in the Parable of the Prodigal Son. When his penitent brother came home and his jubilant father declared a feast of celebration, he angrily refused to join in. Instead of being sour, sullen men, let's go inside and join the party!

Coming Out of the Dark

For many years I lived my life in a minor key. I loved God, loved my wife and children and loved being a Christian, but I had within me a melancholy strain, a vague sorrow that seemed to shadow and haunt my life. I do not know all the reasons why. It can be partly ascribed to my native temperament which tends to the pensive, sensitive side. Some of it originated from a lack of faith and gratitude, some from anger, some from past hurts and some from guilty regret. I came to a deepening realization that this was not the way God wanted me to live and that my dour spirit made life difficult for my wife and children and diminished my effectiveness as a leader.

I decided that I had to change. I saw that Jesus was different from me, and if I meant business about Jesus being my Lord, then he would have to be the Lord of my *personality*. I had to stop accepting the way that I was and allow God to transform my life and heart. I came to believe that, despite how difficult it might be to overcome years of bad habits and joyless attitudes, God could change me.

Accepting Grace

I needed to accept God's grace and love. I had to trust that he had forgiven and forgotten my sins once and for all, taking them from me "as far as the east is from the west" (Psalm 103:12). I needed to rest upon the amazing declarations that "the Lord delights in those...who put their hope in his unfailing love," that I am his "treasured possession" and that he carries me "as a father carries his son" (Psalm 147:11, Exodus 19:5, Deuteronomy 1:31). I think that for many men who were not close to their fathers, who never had a father, who are the children of divorce, or who were abused by their fathers (or some other male authority figure), this is a very difficult matter indeed. We may intellectually acknowledge that we are loved by God but find it difficult to accept or enjoy God's love in a relational or emotional sense. We may believe that God loves us; we just don't think he *likes* us very much! We live under a sense of condemnation, under a cloud of gloom and with a feeling of worthlessness. The only solution is to believe in and embrace God's love for us.

I remember during one period in my life studying Isaiah 40-66 for months, striving to accept the overflowing, abundant, glorious love of God that is described in those pages. I marveled at what I read, but I found it so hard to trust in my heart of hearts what God was telling me. I cannot say that there was one day of breakthrough, but over time, as God continued to speak to me through his word, the light began to dawn and the shadows began to fade.

Today I am a much happier man, because God's love is so much more in my heart and mind. It is partly due to my growing faith, partly due to my maturing over time and partly due to the work of the Holy Spirit, who has poured God's love into my heart (Romans 5:5). Also, after having sons of my own, I can understand so much more the love that God must feel for me as his son. If I am a selfish sinner and love my children so dearly, how much more does God love me!

Despite the Circumstances

The hurts and injustices of life were real joy-stealers for me. They came at me as a young man but intensified as I got older. If life has not yet weighed heavily upon you, it will! Somewhere along the way you will experience the sting of rejection, injustice and disappointment; you will confront the bitterness of failure and lost opportunity. It seems to me that these kinds of defeats and frustrations hit men especially hard, and if we are not careful, they can weigh us down with hurt and bitterness.

I turned to the book of Ecclesiastes for help. Here Solomon addresses life's difficulties and the anger, gloom and frustration that they can bring into our hearts. Studying Solomon's wisdom helped me to see that it is the nature of life in this world to have disappointments and failures and to experience unjust and unloving treatment. Our dearest friends may let us down, and some of them may desert God's kingdom. Church leaders can fail. They can be harsh, uncaring and unthinking. They may go about their business oblivious to our needs, harming us by their sin and ignorance. If we are not spiritual in our mindset, these episodes can so disappoint and embitter us that they rob us of the joy of life.

Solomon tells us to look these events squarely in the face and rejoice and be glad anyway! He teaches us that manhood is not about having life as we wish it but about being strong and joyful in the face of life as it is. We are not promised that life will be just, but that God will be just. Solomon reminds us that we, too, are sinners and have inflicted pain on others. He tells us that God is working out a good plan in the midst of bad circumstances, even when we do not see how. He declares that in the meantime we should have fun and be happy! As I studied, confronted and accepted these realities, and as I saw God's great promises, a joy I had never known began to dawn in my soul.

We must finally see that the issue of joy in life is bigger than our own personal happiness. We must remember that there are those who look to us for guidance and leadership and that we must, for their sakes, be joyful. Our unhappiness may rob them of their birthright of joy. They may begin to feel that serving God is a drudgery and a burden. If you are married, you especially need to realize how your negative emotions can drag down your wife and children. Let it not be so! Let them see us facing our sorrows and difficult days squarely, with eyes that look forward to see the joy that is yet to come. Let them observe us dealing with life's everyday problems with a spirit that sings. Let us banish forever from our hearts the dull, sour and sullen spirit of a man who sighs and moans. Let those around us be inspired by our gladness! Then we will be true mighty men—mighty not only in strength and righteousness, but mighty in the heart of God, which is a heart of exultant joy!

9

DISCIPLINE

But the fruit of the Spirit is...self-control.

Galatians 5:22-23

Without discipline, you will never become a mighty man of God. You may long for honesty, humility and purity with all your heart; you may aspire to be a man of lovingkindness and to experience the joy of God; you may seek courage; but without discipline none of these great qualities will be yours. You may make some progress, you may make some changes, but unless you are disciplined, none of them will last or become permanently etched into your character. Discipline is essential.

The Power of Discipline

All of us have known men whose lives were full of promise. They seemed to have it all: talent, looks, intelligence, personality, opportunity. They seemed to have it all, but they could never put it all together. Even in the church we have known men like this, brothers who we thought would rise to become outstanding men of God but who never reached their potential. Why not? Many times it boils down simply to this: these men lacked discipline.

I can say without equivocation that I have never known a great man who was not supremely disciplined. No man can rise in his profession, build a godly character or grow in his spiritual life without a generous dose of discipline. We might temporarily dazzle our way to the top, we might make a good impression for a period of time, but ultimately, if we are not disciplined, our weaknesses will bring us crashing down in flames.

I can also say that I have never known anyone who was naturally disciplined. Discipline comes easier to some than others, but it is something everyone must work at and work at consciously. I remember well a conversation I had on this subject with Kip McKean, one of the most disciplined men I know. I complimented him on his exemplary discipline and asked him how he did it. He informed me that in spite of the seeming effortlessness of his organization, it was not as easy as it appeared. In words reminding me of Paul's observations in 1 Corinthians 9:27, Kip said, "I have to beat myself and force myself to be disciplined. Most people think it comes easy to me—it doesn't. It is a habit I have worked on for years, and it is something I have to stay on top of all the time." I left that conversation encouraged that I could change and that by tapping the power of the Holy Spirit, anyone else could, too.

Discipline is basically the ability to subordinate. It is the capacity to say yes to the right or best thing, and the ability to say no to the wrong or lesser thing. It is the sign of a mature man, a seasoned man; it is the true hallmark of a mighty man of God and permeates every area of his life.

Permeating Discipline
Mind

We must have a disciplined *mind*. Paul tells us in Romans 8:7 that we must set our minds on the things of the Spirit if we are to be spiritual people. All disciples are indwelt by the Holy Spirit, but not all are under his control. Only those disciples who set their minds on spiritual things become spiritual people. The power to change comes from God, but he places upon us the responsibility of tapping into that power. One key to tapping the power of God is by setting our minds on his word.

Emotions

We must discipline our *emotions*. A man of God must do what he ought to do, not just what he feels like doing. There may be times when anger, discouragement or a bad mood tempts us to be less than the men we should be, but the spirit of manly discipline will cause us to do the right thing.

This is especially true of our moods. Moods are an aspect of our emotional lives that must be brought under the control of our minds and our wills, and ultimately under the lordship of Jesus, if we are ever to become truly disciplined men.

Many of us, though, are accustomed to giving in to our moods. If we wake up feeling a bit discouraged, we allow this feeling to affect our entire day. If we experience some frustration, we give in to irritability as if it were inevitable. We act as if our mood is the ultimate reality—that because we feel a certain way, then that is how we must remain until it passes. How ungodly is this mindset and how contrary to the teaching of the Bible and to the example of Jesus!

Moods are a product of thought, and what we think about is a choice we make.

The solution is simple: to change our mood, we must change the thoughts and attitudes that produced the feelings in the first place.

I am a person who feels things deeply and have had to work hard in learning to discipline my emotions. No man has helped me more to do this than my friend Steve Sapp. Many times when I have found myself in a passionate frame of mind, he has helped me to contain my feelings and direct them into a productive and holy path. At other times, he has helped me see that my emotions, though strong, were selfish and misdirected, and that if I gave in to them, I would at best be making a mistake, or at worst, sinning. I am deeply grateful for Steve's influence in my life, and if you are a man of deep feeling, I would urge you to value, cultivate and listen to friends who help you discipline your emotions.

Desires

We must discipline our *desires*. Included are the appetites for food, for sex and for pleasure. None of these desires are wrong in and of themselves, but are wrong when they are dominated by selfishness rather than the will of God. Discipline will enable us to keep our appetites on a leash—the leash of righteousness.

Schedule

We must discipline our *time*. All men possess the same amount of time. It is how each man uses his time that determines his ultimate impact. If you fritter away your time, your life will be a waste. If you do not learn how to organize your time, you will be overwhelmed by your responsibilities. Many of us could do more, but our refusal to bring our time under the lordship of Christ holds us back. Purchase some sort of daily calendar—be it old-fashioned or high tech—and get in the habit of using it. Set aside a few minutes at the beginning of every day to plan your schedule. I find that the best time for me to tackle this task is right after my quiet time, when I am most spiritually attuned. I have made it my habit to go immediately from my time of prayer and Bible study to planning my day. I have found that this brings God into the details of my schedule and that I am able to take on the challenges before me with a much greater sense of God's presence and power.

After many years of effort, I have developed my own daily planning sheets that are uniquely adapted to my lifestyle and responsibilities. I have them programmed into my computer and have learned, after practice, to use my system well. It has saved me countless frustrations and has delivered me from inefficiency and failure. I would urge you to either develop your own system, or to utilize one of the many excellent systems available on the market. This will take determination and persistence, but the rewards are immeasurable! Remember, even the best time-management system in the world will do you no good unless you use it *every day*, and unless you consult it frequently *throughout the day*.

I urge you, do not waste another day being undisciplined with your time. Make a decision to change, and do not quit until you have mastered it!

Surroundings

We must discipline our *environment*. You cannot become a mighty man if you live in an environment of chaos. Look at your work area, your desk, your closet, your garage—are these areas organized, or are they cluttered and messy? God is not a God of confusion but of order. If we are to be godly men, then we must bring order into our surroundings. Gain a solid conviction about this, then start where you are. Clean up your desk. Create a simple file-folder system for your bills, records and other papers. Go into your closet and throw out all the junk and old clothes you have been hoarding. (If you are married, get ready to get a big hug from your wife!) Notice how much better you feel. And don't you enjoy all those great compliments you get from the disorganized, messy people around you?

Enemies of Discipline

There are three enemies of discipline that deserve our special attention.

The first is *procrastination*. The undisciplined man is often characterized by this common, but deadly, fault. Putting off what we need to do is a habit we can and must break. When Abraham was told by God to go and sacrifice his son Isaac, we read that he got up "early the next morning" (Genesis 22:3) to carry out this trying assignment. If we learn to tackle difficult tasks early in the day, then we find that we are less burdened and more full of joy, and that we get more done. The man who delays the onerous and unpleasant task is only making things harder for himself.

The second enemy of discipline, *indecision,* is closely related to the first. Many of us, when confronted by the numerous options, cannot bring ourselves to make a decision. We fret, fume and worry. The longer we wait, the harder and more complicated the task and the decision become. When deciding important matters, we must not rush, to be sure. We must seek God's will in prayer, study, providence and in wisdom from spiritual friends. But for many of us, we delay too long in making decisions, and we will not be firm once we have made them.

Lateness is the third enemy. We are late getting out of bed, late going to bed, late for appointments, late for work, late for class, late for church, late in paying our bills. We may be only a little late, but we are late nonetheless. Some of us feel badly about it and fret and fume all the way to our next late arrival. Others of us have little or no conscience about our tardiness, but those around us must bear the consequences of our lateness.

To conquer this terrible weakness, we must move it from the realm of being a minor offense to one that is laid at the feet of selfishness, pride, rudeness and laziness. When we look at our tardiness in this light, we will finally see it for what it is.

Let me offer several practical suggestions to overcome this weakness.

1. Gain a conviction that lateness is selfishness and sin. This will increase your motivation to conquer it.

2. Stop overpreparing. Many of us are late because we cannot resist doing one more task before we go out the door. To conquer this, try having everything ready in advance, then you will not be caught trying to get ready to go at the last minute and under pressure.

3. Give yourself a generous margin of time. Some men, in the name of efficiency, try to live by split-second timing. Life is too full of the unexpected for this plan to work. The last-minute delay, congested traffic, a conversation on the way out the door—all these and more seemingly conspire against a closely timed schedule. If you, like me, are a chronic underestimator of time, just add a few minutes to everything you plan to do, and you will find you start arriving on time, without fuming and fussing.

The only way to become a disciplined person is by making it a habitual part of our character. We must become so disciplined that it finally becomes second nature. But this is not easy. It usually takes about two weeks to begin a new habit and about six more weeks to make it a standard part of our lives. At first the change seems awkward, and the temptation is to quit in discouragement. Then, if we manage to get through the difficult first two weeks, our tendency will be to lose focus and slip back into our old ways again. This is when it is critical to stay with our new habit! Once you establish it, it will become your lifetime friend and ally.

I used to fail to get up on time in the morning. I would set an alarm, but after it went off, I would lay in bed for a few (or many!) minutes before getting up. When I did finally get out of bed, I would be in a rush, be angry with myself, feel guilty for blowing it (again!) and lose my sense of joy and confidence for the day. Not a pretty picture! I finally came up with the two-alarm system, wherein I set a radio alarm on my nightstand, and set another loud and unpleasant alarm across the room, timed to go off five minutes later. It worked! It got me out of bed on time, and I enjoyed the change so much that I have maintained this habit into my adult life. This is but one example of how to break a pesky bad habit, to encourage you to use your head—and your heart—to make the needed changes in your discipline. May your habits become a blessing, and not a curse in your life!

Two Keys

The two keys to becoming a disciplined man of God are *conviction* and *determination*. Most people I know who are not disciplined do not have a great conviction about it. Others claim that they have tried to become disciplined, but that it is simply beyond their powers. They have given up, taking the attitude of "I guess I just don't have what it takes to be disciplined." The truth is, *everyone* has the ability to become disciplined. If you see the need, and if you are willing to stay with it, discipline will eventually become a way of life for you. You simply must continue to try until what now seems awkward becomes habitual and natural.

A world of newfound accomplishment awaits you. Decide that you will tap into the power of God to help you and that you will forever leave behind your old life of laziness, disorganization and failure. Become a disciplined, mighty man of God!

For God did not give us a spirit of timidity, but a spirit of power, of love and of self-discipline. (2 Timothy 1:7)

PART 2

THE FRONTIERS OF MANHOOD

10

EMOTION

Jesus wept.

John 11:35

Most men are baffled and confused when it comes to their emotions. They are unexplored, unknown and unfamiliar territory. Although some men are deeply emotional, for many others quite the opposite is true. They either do not feel deeply, or will not *let* themselves feel deeply. For them, emotion is the undesirable domain of women, children and weak or effeminate men. In their view, the word "emotional" itself is a rebuke and a censure. "Oh, he's just the emotional type" is an ascription of weakness, shame and failure. Men with this belief pride themselves in being souls of pure, unalloyed logic and reason. They confidently claim to use their minds, uncluttered by feelings, to direct their affairs. They disdain emotion as an impediment to the application of fact and intellect. They often have little identification with or use for those who live in the realm of feeling.

Consider the great men of the Bible. They were emotional and passionate—they believed deeply, and thus they felt deeply. Look at Moses, the fervent, fiery prophet who led the Hebrews out of slavery. Think about David, Israel's singer of songs, the man after God's own heart, who shed tears with his friend Jonathan as they parted when David went into exile. Read about David's intense repentance as recorded in Psalm 51, in which he pours out to God his confession of adultery, murder and lying. You can feel the burning shame of his heart even now, thousands of years after he wrote the words. Reflect on Peter, who, shortly after his denial of Jesus, looked into the eyes of his Lord and "went out and wept bitterly" (Matthew 26:75). Contemplate Paul, the hardened, self-assured Pharisee who had such drive and determination that it would seem no tender feeling could ever find lodgment in his breast, who, after becoming a disciple of Jesus, wrote, "For I wrote you out of great distress and anguish of heart and with many tears" (2 Corinthians 2:4).

These are some of the greatest heroes in the Bible, and to a man, they were men who felt and expressed deep emotion. From their examples we can readily see that passion is not only a good quality but is an essential characteristic of the fully developed mighty man of God. It is a quality he must both seek and possess.

But this is not the complete picture. As important as it is for us to become men of deeper feeling, we know that emotion and passion have another side that is dangerous and sinister. Unbridled, unrighteous emotion has been the downfall of many a man. We need to examine this elusive, crucial theme more thoroughly. What should be the role of emotion in the life of a man?

Understanding Emotion

Emotion is "a mental condition of feeling, excitement or passion." It involves the stirring of our sensibilities and can involve physiological changes such as laughter, tears or nervousness. Although someone in an emotional state may engage in behavior that at first glance appears irrational, emotion is usually a product of thought and can be logically understood.

However, this is not to say that there are situations when emotion seemingly has no logical basis. Usually these situations involve drug usage, physical illness or injury, hormonal imbalance or mental or emotional derangement. Emotion can be heightened by our physical condition (i.e., exhaustion) or by our environment (i.e. music, light/darkness, colors, weather). It can be influenced by our body chemistry (i.e. drugs, ıones) in dramatic ways. But even in these cases, some rational contributing or underlying cause of an emotional condition can be discerned. Although emotion involves feeling and passion, it is inextricably linked to our minds.

Emotions or Logic?

Is it best to be emotional or logical? Is there a time to heed one and ignore the other? Or is there a balance between the two for which we should always strive?

Perhaps the best way to answer these questions is to consider the marriage relationship. Love is the rational commitment I have made to my wife, to be faithful to her for life—in sickness and in health, for richer or for poorer—until death separates us. It is a decision I honor regardless of my emotional state. There may be times when I don't feel like giving, or when I would prefer to be selfish, but I have made a decision of will to love my wife, and I keep that promise regardless of my mood. The man who bases his conduct in marriage solely upon emotion will be an unreliable, undependable spouse; he will be a good or bad husband according to his mood.

But, to be complete, my love for my wife must go beyond commitment and loyalty. It must include the emotions of warmth I feel as we share life together and as I reflect upon what she means to me. If my love is a love consisting only of duty, and if I have little or no emotion within me, something is missing in my heart and in my marriage as well.

Godly love blends commitment with feeling. The man who makes a commitment to be faithful to his wife, but does not combine it with a passionate, warm devotion to her will find her becoming increasingly unhappy and emotionally starved. Our wives need us to do more than help provide for their physical and financial needs; they need emotional nurturing. They need to feel our love, not just know that we are loyal. Love means much more than just living under the same roof and helping to pay the bills! Our wives want to know that we feel passionately about them, that our feelings for them are deep, exciting and romantic. They want to know that they make us happy, that we thoroughly enjoy being with them.

Our lack of emotional expression not only hurts our wives but our children as well. Children are not creatures of reason, but of feeling! To be close to us, they need to bond with us emotionally. They need to see our emotional side. They will appreciate more deeply a time of laughter with us, or a time when we shed tears in front of them, than another one of our long, logical lectures. I remember crying in front of my son David as I apologized to him for my insensitivity during a time of sadness and struggle in his life. Those tears did more to tell him how much I cared and to bond us together than anything I could have said. On another occasion, as we prayed before he left for school, I wept as I expressed my gratitude for him during the prayer. My son still vividly remembers these and other similar moments, years after they happened. Expressions of manly emotion deeply impress children. Never underestimate how much you and your children need those times! If you have failed to convey to them your emotions, your relationship with your children is not as close as it should be, and they do not feel your love as they should. Humble yourself, let down your guard, and become a more emotional, expressive father!

The answer to our earlier question, whether it is good to be emotional or to be reasonable, is yes! Yes, we must be men of reason and loyalty, and yes, we must be men of passion and feeling!

Righteous—or Not?

How can we know when emotion is right or wrong? Let us consider the following examples.

Moses was angry when he came down from Mount Sinai to find the Israelites worshiping a golden calf. He was so incensed that he threw down and broke into pieces the tablets of the Ten Commandments. He then ground up the offensive golden calf, scattered the ashes in the water supply and told the rebellious tribes to drink it. On another occasion, at Meribah, Moses was confronted by the people complaining of their hardships and saying they wished they had never left Egypt. God tells Moses to speak to a rock in their presence that he might bring water out of it to quench their thirst. Moses does not do as God tells him, but in anger he strikes the rock with his staff.

Moses was angry on both of these occasions; how did God view them? There was no censure given Moses by God for his anger at Mount Sinai. It was justified and was righteous. But that was not the case at Meribah. There, his anger was selfish and sinful. The years of struggle, complaining and rebellion by the Hebrews finally overcame him. The Bible says that "rash words came from Moses' lips" (Psalms 106:3). God rebuked Moses for his prideful loss of temper and because of it forbade him from entering the promised land.

What are the lessons for us? Emotion can be right or wrong. It is right when it is motivated by a righteous purpose and results in righteous conduct, but is wrong when motivated by sinful purposes and results in sinful deeds. When we act within God's commands and are motivated by a desire to uphold God's name and honor, then anger can be justified. However, if we are acting out of frustration, resentment and personal hurt, we are wrong.

Emotions Examined

Fear

Fear is one of the most powerful and prevalent emotions. It is motivated by a desire to protect ourselves or others from danger. Fear of God is good. Those who do not respect and honor God as their Creator and Judge are foolish and will live to regret it. "The fear of the Lord is the beginning of wisdom," says Solomon in the book of Proverbs (1:7). A healthy reverence for God and fear of his judgment can save our souls. But fear can also harm us. We can fear the opinions of men more than the judgment of God. We can fear that obeying God will harm us or that we will fail him if we were to try. Anxiety is fear of what might go wrong in the future. It can debilitate us and take away our joy in life. Being overwhelmed and burdened is another form of fear. We fear that we will not get everything done, that our work and responsibilities are too great. We feel pressured, overburdened. Again, our emotions can so grip us that we exaggerate our problems or become so anxious that we can no longer tackle and solve them.

A man controlled by fear must realize the impact his fear is having on him and on those close to him. Fear confines many a man to a life of small and limited influence. It also keeps him from enjoying life with his wife and children and from helping them to overcome their own fears. As a husband and father, you are the head of your household. The leader in any situation is called upon to have courage and inspire it in others. When you are in the grip of fear, you are a weakening, discouraging influence on your family. Realize the problems you are causing under your own roof, and become a man of courage!

Anger

We have already seen that anger can be good or bad. Righteous anger for God's honor is good. Anger when the rights of the weak are trampled by the strong is good. But anger is a dangerous emotion and must be carefully monitored. Paul wrote, "In your anger do not sin. Do not let the sun go down on your anger" (Ephesians 4:26). We are forbidden to let our anger get out of control, and we are not allowed to let our anger go unresolved. The explosive anger of selfish passion and the brooding anger of bitterness are sins we must overcome. Anger can also show itself in sinful sarcasm, ridicule and cutting remarks. It can reveal itself in withdrawal from others. Unrighteous anger shows itself when we are frustrated, irritable, edgy and cranky.

A man who gives in to outbursts of rage destroys his closest relationships. His associates and friends are forever wary of his eruptions. His wife and children live in fear of him. His caustic words and violent behaviors can do physical and emotional damage that can hardly be repaired. The man who loses his temper usually does not realize the damage he is doing. He may feel better after letting off steam, but those he has scalded continue to bear the hurt, fear, resentment and bitterness of his rage. He may never fully know how severely he has undercut the confidence of those who are his victims, nor the emotional and spiritual damage he has caused them. Such a man needs to come to conviction of his wrongs, beg the forgiveness of his family and friends, and most of all, forever forsake his sinful anger.

Other men carry their anger more discreetly. They would never think of blowing up, but they are deeply angry nonetheless. Behind their placid exteriors a furnace is burning. Theirs is the anger of brooding and bitterness. Theirs is the anger of simmering resentment and malice. Such men hold grudges. When they are hurt, they do not forgive; when they are offended, they do not reconcile. These men become depressed. It is my observation that perpetually depressed men are usually angry men. They too make life miserable for their friends and families. Their loved ones do not understand why they are down, or why they would rather sulk than enjoy life. Sometimes these men let out their anger by becoming critical of their families. Their wives and children are forever in a state of consternation, wondering what they have done to make these men unhappy with them. They do not realize it is not their fault, but that they are suffering undeservedly at the hands of someone who carries deep within him a sinful, unresolved anger.

The man of brooding anger must face his sin, just as the man of passionate rage must face his. He must realize the horrible penalties his bitterness is exacting upon him and those he loves. He must confess his anger, resolve it, and clear his heart of the bitterness that is eating away at the very core of his soul. No anger is worth ruining your life or the lives of those you love!

Guilt

Guilt is the inner feeling of condemnation by our conscience, the sense of self-judgment, that renders a verdict of disapproval on our actions. In spite of the discomfort they bring us, our guilty feelings serve a good purpose. Without a sensitive conscience, we will not feel a sense of God's disapproval when we sin against him. Indeed, without a tender conscience that brings conviction to our souls, we cannot be saved.

But again, guilt is an emotion that needs spiritual discipline. We can have an oversensitive conscience that unjustly condemns us. We can feel terrible guilt over legalistic matters that are not very important to God. We can continue to feel guilty for sins for which God has forgiven us. We can feel guilt over matters for which we are not responsible.

Our consciences are God given instruments, but they must be educated. Our consciences can mislead us if our moral compass is not true. On the one hand, we must be keenly sensitive to sin, and on the other, we must never let our consciences become seared and unresponsive. The solution is to accurately set our consciences according to the teachings of God's word. And when we are confronted with matters where the righteous path may not be readily apparent, it is helpful to consult mature friends who can help us make objective, wise judgments.

Gaining Control of Our Emotions

Self-control is nowhere more needed than in governing our emotions. Untamed passion must not be allowed to dominate our lives, but must be brought under the rule of God's word and under the mastery of the lordship of Jesus. We have just seen how our sinful anger, no matter how deeply felt, must be confessed and repented of. So must our other unrighteous emotions be overcome.

On those occasions when Jesus said to the apostles, "Do not be afraid," he meant what he said. He intended that they collect their runaway emotions and be courageous. When God told Joshua, "Do not be discouraged" (Joshua 1:9), he meant that Joshua was to not allow himself to be emotionally down. God had in mind that Joshua should not permit the great task of conquering the promised land to daunt him or turn him back. Is not discouragement merely fear that has set in for the long term?

When John tells the believers, "we set our hearts at rest in his presence whenever our hearts condemn us. For God is greater than our hearts" (1 John 3:20), is he not saying that unruly, emotional guilt must be decisively rejected?

Emotion can be controlled, and it must be controlled. Feelings are not the ultimate reality—God's truth is the ultimate reality, and feelings must be brought under the control of the will of God.

Developing Our Emotions

Having said all this, let us close with a challenge for the mighty man of God to become a man of deep and righteous emotion.

Heartfelt Compassion

We need to learn to feel with others as Jesus did. A surefire means to arrest the attention of Jesus was to come to him in tears. Whether it was the grieving mother who lost her only son (Luke 7:11ff) or the penitent prostitute in tears (Luke 7:36ff), Jesus felt for those who were hurting and emotionally distraught. He wept with his friend Mary at her brother's graveside, even though he knew that in only a few moments he would bring Lazarus back to life and turn her tears into tears of joy (John 11:32-35). He was moved to cry simply because he cared for her and longed to share her grief.

Many of us hold back our tears. We are too proud to cry. We don't want to embarrass ourselves. We don't want to appear weak. Or, it may be that we genuinely do not feel. We are too hard-hearted, too logical, too analytical, too distant from others to cry for them and with them. If this is the case with you, I would urge you to not let fear and pride hold you back any longer. Let yourself feel with and for others. Walk in their footsteps; look into their souls. Let your heart and your feelings be open to those around you.

Begin Today

Some of you may want to change, but don't know quite what you need to do or how to get started. First, we must understand that some of us will never be as emotional as others. Don't worry, even if feeling and expressing emotion doesn't come easily for you, you can still grow in these areas. If you have difficulty verbalizing deep feelings, I would urge you to try writing them down in a card. Some of us who are tongue-tied in person turn eloquent with a pen in our hands! In learning to feel and express more, I would encourage simple and unsophisticated attempts. Don't get hung up on thinking you have to say something profound—just be honest! Others will appreciate your efforts, no matter how clumsy and halting you may feel they are. And you will be amazed at how quickly you improve as you continue to try! You will also be so encouraged by the responses you get back, that you will be more and more motivated to become an expressive man.

In becoming more expressive with your wife, I would urge you to get jump-started by going a bit overboard. Give her a nice gift, send her flowers and include with them a card in which you passionately express your feelings for her. Go for it! If she thinks you are going a little bonkers, so what? What's she going to do—walk out on you? I don't think so! After she overcomes her initial shock that you, her nominee for the next stone face on Mount Rushmore, have spoken words of passion to her, she will start loving it!

Intimacy with God

The best way I know for men to develop emotionally is by drawing near to God. To do that, you are going to have to invest some time. I would urge you to make it your practice to go away as often as needed for extended time alone with him. The example of Jesus, the teaching of the Scriptures, the testimony of many other men and my own personal experience confirms that this practice is absolutely essential if men are going to grow emotionally. We men are so task oriented that if we do not take time away from our responsibilities, we will never learn to feel. We will go on with our routines as if we are devoid of emotion, but in reality, our feelings are just buried deep within us. If we do not encourage them to emerge, they will atrophy and eventually die. As we grow older, we will become men who are increasingly dull, lifeless and empty. Don't let this happen to you! Take the time to be with God and to grow emotionally.

Some Personal Examples

When I went away to write this book, I experienced one of those times of great emotion in my life. As I was packing to leave on Sunday afternoon, my daughter Elizabeth came to my study to give me a Valentine's day gift. I opened the package to behold a photograph of her. I don't know what it was—perhaps the camera caught her expression in such a way that showed all that I love and admire about her; perhaps it was knowing that in a few weeks she would be getting married; perhaps it was fatherly pride that she is so beautiful; perhaps it was sheer gratitude that I have a wonderful daughter who loves me so dearly, and whom I love so dearly—whatever the reason, as I looked at the picture, I felt a deep surge of emotion rise within me. I hugged Elizabeth and broke down crying. It was all I knew to do. I had no words to express my feelings. I managed to say "Thank you," before she left. As long as I live, I will remember all that that moment meant to me and all that I felt but could not say to her in words.

Later that day my friend Mitch Mitchell drove me down to the North Carolina coast where I caught the ferry to take me to the island where I was to be alone and work on this book. The beginning of the new year had been difficult. A dear friend had fallen away from the church and in doing so had deeply hurt our congregation and my family. There was also before me the challenge of getting the church up and running for the new year and the daunting task of writing this book.

When I arrived on the island, I unpacked my things and went for a walk on the beach. It was a beautiful, cold, clear winter day. The sun was setting over the water as I stood just where the Cape Fear River empties itself into the Atlantic ocean. As I stepped onto the beach, I immediately felt the burdens rise off my shoulders. I felt immense relief to be there, alone with God. I was overwhelmed and in awe of the majestic, unhurried, lonely beauty all around me. The waves rolled on the beach. The sun put on a dazzling show of orange, red, blue, purple, gray, silver and white as it sank slowly into the sea. I wept; I cried; I sobbed. Not tears of sadness, not tears of sorrow, but tears of joy, praise and celebration. All I could think to say to God were the words spoken by Peter on the mount of the transfiguration: "Lord, it is good to be here!" Over and over I said them, simply thankful that I was in such a beautiful place, alone with God, and that I would be there with him for several days to enjoy his company and do his work.

Later that week on Thursday evening, I came back out to the beach at sunset. This day marked my thirtieth spiritual birthday, the anniversary of the day when, as a nineteen-year-old college sophomore I made my decision to follow Jesus and was baptized into him. That evening, I thanked God for my salvation and prayed through the years of my life. I was absolutely overwhelmed with gratitude as the memories of years of service to God swept through my soul. Old friends, great moments of victory, recoveries from horrible defeats, the gifts of my wife, my children, my friends in the kingdom; the ways God had led and comforted me, the times he had reached down and saved me again and again, the ways he had shaped and molded my character; the blessings of my life in the here and now.

I tried repeatedly to leave the beach and get back to my work, but felt compelled to turn back to pray some more. The tears flowed freely. I didn't try to stop them. I fell to my knees in adoration and praise. I raised my hands in thanksgiving. I raised my voice to be heard above the howling wind and crashing surf. I felt that this must be a small part of what we must feel one day when we are with God in heaven and see his face. The Scriptures tell us that God gives us special times like this in which the Holy Spirit witnesses with our spirits that we are the children of God. We need these moments, and we should not fear them. This was one of the greatest occurrences of emotion, joy and ecstasy in my life, and I will be forever grateful for it.

I tell these stories to encourage you to become a man who lets out his emotions. I would urge you to let your emotions develop, to neither quench them nor hold them back, to stop being a man so tightly wound, a man so much in control, a man with your life so ordered and constricted. Many of us long for emotional freedom but are afraid of it. We fear what we might find. Don't worry—you will only find a part of your soul that has been too long dormant, too long sleeping, too long confined; you will find a part of you that needs to be freed and released. Under the influence of the life-giving power of the Holy Spirit, and the warmth of the love of God, let yourself without shame come fully alive, a man who knows how to feel!

FRIENDSHIP

> *Jonathan said to David, "Go in peace, for we have sworn friendship with each other in the name of the LORD, saying, 'The LORD is witness between you and me, and between your descendants and my descendants forever.'" Then David left, and Jonathan went back to the town.*

> 1 Samuel 20:42

Is not life all about relationships? The people we love and who love us in return are what give joy, meaning and fulfillment to us. A man's life can be measured by the quality and numbers of his friends. And while friendship is one of life's greatest treasures and joys, loneliness is one of its most awful miseries.

Some people think women are the ones who need friends, and men are the independent, distant, shallow types who just need buddies—buddies to hang out with, to play with, to work with, but not to share their hearts with. I am sure that there is some truth to this stereotype, but to say or believe that men do not need each other is to make a serious mistake, the mistake of a lifetime.

Men need deep friendships because God made us that way. "A man of many companions may come to ruin, but there is a friend who sticks closer than a brother" (Proverbs 18:24). Many men want only shallow relationships. But true friendship means that someone knows us—that they know what we think, what we feel and who we really are. Certainly we share fun, laughter and work with our friends, but true friendship must go deeper than those things.

Why We Need Friends

Strength

We need friends to strengthen us. "And Saul's son Jonathan went to David at Horesh and helped him find strength in God" (1 Samuel 23:16). Here we find David at one of the lowest points of his life. He had been driven from his home in disgrace and shame. He needed God and he needed a deeper faith; he needed a friend. Jonathan came to him and helped him draw nearer to God. Perhaps they prayed together, perhaps Jonathan reminded him of God's promises given to him when Samuel the prophet anointed him king years before.

Comfort

We need friends to comfort us. Paul says that we need to learn to comfort others with the comfort we have received from God (2 Corinthians 1:4). Many of us fail miserably here. We are not sympathetic. We do not feel with and for others, and we do not know how to stand alongside them in their hour of need. Perhaps we need to learn how to cry with someone, to let our tears flow as theirs do. Perhaps we need to be the first to cry. For example, David and Jonathan shed tears together, and Paul cried as he wrote his letters. I would say that if another man has not seen you cry, your relationship is not that close. If you say to yourself, "I'm just not the emotional type," then you are denying the lordship of Jesus in this area of your life, because Jesus was an emotional man who showed his feelings in front of his closest friends (Matthew 26:37-38).

Advice

We need friends to advise us. "Perfume and incense bring joy to the heart, and the pleasantness of one's friend springs from his earnest counsel" (Proverbs 27:9). Friends give us their wisdom and advice in the great and small matters of life. Men are often too proud to seek advice. We feel that this is a sign of weakness, that it will cause others to lose respect for us or that it will give others the license to run our lives. This kind of thinking is unspiritual, ungodly and worldly. It will deny us one of the great sources of God's guidance in our lives.

I make it my practice to frequently seek the counsel of other men. I ask advice on anything of importance—from how to spend my time to how to spend my money; from buying a house to where I send my kids to school; from how I can grow spiritually to how I can better build my church; all of these and more, do I lay before my friends. I cannot say how many times the advice of brothers has spared me from the worst of mistakes. Nor can I say how much the wise counsel of other men has guided me into some of the very best decisions of my life. I have at times neglected the advice of friends and paid a terrible price. I have also known men who called me their close friend but who never really let me advise them or be privy to their decisions. Such men were fooling themselves—we were not, and are not, deeply close to each other.

Correction

We need friends to correct and rebuke us. "Wounds from a friend can be trusted, but an enemy multiplies kisses" (Proverbs 27:6). Your best friends must tell you the truth, even when it is hard for you to take it. Advice is one thing, correction and rebuke are another. Rebuke is a strong reprimand, a dressing down, a laying it out and telling it like it is! I often think how much better it would have been for King David if Nathan or another friend had seen the signs of his spiritual decline and confronted him with them before he committed adultery with Bathsheba, rather than afterward. But Nathan at least had the love and courage to approach David when no one else did. It takes a mighty man to tell his friend he is in sin or that he is in the wrong, even at the risk of losing the friendship—but it must be done!

Companions

We need friends as our companions. Life is hard, challenging and often very serious. We need other men to share it with us. We need them to be by our side as we face both the hum-drum and intense moments of life. We need them to help lighten our load as they share with us the times of fun, laughter and recreation. We also need their companionship in our darkest hours. We cannot know all that Jesus felt on his final night in the Garden of Gethsemane, but we know that in that dismal hour he desperately wanted the companionship of his closest friends.

The Marks of Friendship

Honesty

True friendship requires honesty. We cannot be close to someone we do not know and who does not know us. For another man to know you, you will have to open your heart and let him inside. Simply being around someone is not enough. Yes, we learn about others by observation and by spending time with them—and we learn things that talking will not reveal to us—but as God had to speak his words to us for us to know him, so we will have to speak our hearts to others for them to know us.

To know each other at a soul level, you will have to let your friend know the *facts*, not only the current events of your life, but also your personal history—your childhood, family background, and the life-shaping events as well. Your friend will need to know your *opinions*—what you really think, believe and hold in your mind. Many of us are afraid that if someone knew what we really thought, they would not want to be our friend anymore. Such an attitude will keep you forever distant from other men, forever insecure and forever wearing a mask. Your friend will have to know your *feelings*. Are you angry, sad, discouraged, happy, anxious, guilty...? If you hide your emotions away from another man, he cannot know you. Last, there must be *mutual* openness for there to be true friendship. If both people are not devoted to openness and honesty, then there is not real friendship. There are relationships of leader-follower, employer-employee, counselor-counselee, but these are not necessarily relationships of friendship. There may even be genuine love and admiration in such associations, but that is not the same as friendship.

Devotion

There must be devotion to one another for there to be friendship. Devotion means that we stick with someone for the long haul, that we are faithful friends for a lifetime. I decided long ago that whatever my other weaknesses and flaws, I would not fail in friendship. I realized that to have friends, you must first be a friend. I decided to pour my life into my friends. I resolved to do my best to be available, loyal, open and faithful to them. Now, when one of us moves away, I strive to keep up with them. I call, fax and write them. I also pray for them regularly, and for many on a daily basis. I cannot keep up with everyone as I would like—but I keep up with some very regularly, and many others as much as I can. We may rarely see one another, and may never again live in the same place, but we can still open our hearts and express our deepest thoughts and feelings to one another. Such is the joy of true friendship. Such is the greatness of having other men in your life, men who are and always will be, your friends!

But even the best of friendships are not perfect. Devotion is the quality of hanging with a friend when you learn the worst about them and when you see them sin, fail and make mistakes. It is the quality that continues to love and to desire closeness even when the other man has hurt you, let you down and disappointed you. If you withdraw from other men whenever you are hurt or disappointed, then you will never have them as friends. You must work through such conflicts with honesty, love and patience, knowing that the reward of a deeper and truer friendship awaits you.

What if you feel you have been open, that you have sought a close relationship, but the other man is unresponsive or disinterested? Let me say clearly that we cannot force our friendship upon anyone. Friendship is a gift another person gives you. There are times, however, that try though we may to build a friendship, the other person will not respond. Perhaps this man is not capable of the depth of friendship that we seek. Perhaps he is too busy. Perhaps he is afraid of closeness. Perhaps he has something to hide. Perhaps he just is not drawn to us. When this happens, we are sorely tempted to be hurt, angry or embittered. It is a painful thing to extend our friendship and have our efforts fall flat.

What are we to do? We have to pick ourselves up, get back on the track and keep on running! Remember that while love is commanded, friendship is a bit more magical. I have wasted time and energy in my life wishing for some guys to be my friends. All I did was become weary and lose confidence! In the meantime, I overlooked the other men around me who were eager for my friendship. When I stopped trying to force relationships, and continued to act in a friendly, caring manner, some of those guys eventually became my close friends. Others have not, and probably never will. But life is too short and God is too good for you to waste time worrying over a failed attempt at friendship!

Expression

To have friends, you must become an expressive man. By this I mean more than plain honesty; I mean expressing your feelings of admiration, respect and love for your friend. As men, we are often leery of telling another man that we need him. The brothers to whom I am the closest are those to whom I have expressed my feelings most deeply, and they to me. It is pride and fear that keep us from being this way. Even as you read this, some of you fear that if you were this open, it might show weakness, that you might look foolish or that perhaps you would be considered effeminate or to have homosexual tendencies. Read through the letters of Paul in the New Testament, and you will find him to be a strong man who was unafraid to express to his friends his deepest feelings and needs. One of my best friends, Reese Neyland, never writes me a letter or card in which he does not close with the verse found at the heading of this chapter, the verse that says that Jonathan and David had sworn friendship to each other for life. There is a deep love between us; we are like blood brothers. We have shed tears as we have discussed those feelings, and as we have written each other about them. The fact that men deny themselves this kind of expression is one reason their relationships are so shallow. We have a warped sense of masculinity and sexuality if we think that tears, affection and the expression of deep gratitude are reserved for women, for weak men, for homosexuals or for the most intense moments of life—sickness, the death of a loved one, or a winning touchdown!

Generosity

This is one of the greatest requirements of friendship. When Jonathan gave his heart to David, he also gave him some of his most prized and meaningful possessions: his robe, tunic, sword, bow and belt (1 Samuel 18:1-4). If you want friends, give. First and foremost, give of yourself; then give gifts. Friends cannot be purchased by gifts or money, but there is no friendship without generosity. And that generosity will involve the gifts of our time, our attention and our possessions. Stingy, thoughtless men do not have friends. If you do not give gifts—birthday gifts or other types—prepare for a life without many friends!

Gifts are the tangible expressions of our love. They are the ways we leave someone with a definite expression and remembrance of us and our friendship. They serve as a symbol of all that the person means to us. It says something about your friendship when someone remembers your birthday—and so does forgetting it! You may dismiss it by telling yourself, "Well, I'm sure it just slipped his mind," but it still means something is missing. I am not saying that you must exchange birthday gifts every year to be friends, but I am saying that this type of relationship lacks the closeness it could have.

I do not get to see or talk to my friend Kip McKean that often, but ever since we have known each other, we have consistently exchanged birthday gifts. Each year, several days before my birthday, I find in my mailbox Kip's present and card. In spite of being separated for most of the more than twenty-five years of our relationship, our mutual remembrance has played an important role in keeping our friendship alive and growing.

Expanding Our Friendships

We must realize we will have different kinds of friends and different levels of closeness. Friendships vary according to the complexities of the human heart and to the intricacies of shared experiences. Give all you can, and let the friendship grow and be guided by God. Some friendships will be like that of David and Jonathan: there will be an almost magical bonding of your souls; you will "click" easily and immediately with one another. Other friendships will grow over time.

We need older friends to mentor and guide us. We need friends who are our peers and who share our hobbies, sense of humor, likes and dislikes. We need men as our friends who are very different than we, who have different temperaments and personalities. Some of us have chosen only to be close to men similar to us. If we are a sportsman, we have no intellectual or artsy friends. If we are a mathematical, engineering type, we limit ourselves to fellow computer jockeys. If we are tough and unemotional, we disrespect and avoid men who are more sensitive. How foolish, how prideful, how limiting! I think of the men in my life who are so very different than me, and how much richness, challenge and perspective they have brought me, and I would not trade those friendships for anything in the world!

Do you have any friends of another race? If you do not, then you may be a racist, or at least you are suffering from being locked in your own small world. Being raised in the southern United States in the 1950s and early 1960s meant that I, as a white, was socially separated from blacks. When I came into God's kingdom in 1969, that immediately began to change, and I am eternally grateful! Getting to know and love many men of color in the church has radically altered the worldly mindset I grew up with and has given me a respect, affection and insight I never had before. This is true of those who are black, Hispanic, Asian, Native American and those of other races who have befriended me and whom I have befriended. These friendships have enriched, changed and elevated my life immensely. I sometimes look back on my earlier years and think how ignorant, foolish and limited a human being I was in those days. As I observe men who are confined to a small world with a limited viewpoint on other races, cultures and types of people, I can only thank God for letting me be in a worldwide spiritual family that has given me friendships I would never have known otherwise!

A lifetime provides us the amazing opportunity to forge friendships with countless different people, and each friendship will be unique. You sometimes are given the gift of friendship when you seemingly make no effort at all—such a gift is rare, and when it is given us, we should deeply appreciate it. Other friendships grow with time and experience. Some of the best friends we can have are those that come after months and years of working side by side, and as the time passes, the shared victories, defeats, and experiences draw us together. Other friendships are ones that we initiate—that we work for and give ourselves to, and are rewarded by a responsive heart.

I want to close this chapter with a few lines from a song written some years ago by my friend Dave Graham. He wrote it as an expression of our friendship as I was moving to another city, and I share it with you with a prayer that you will have, and be, a friend like this:

Old friends never die; old friends never die.
Just as sure as the sun, it'll cross that big ol' sky,
Old friends never die.
I'll see you soon, my friend, on the other side.
Cause old friends, old friends like you,
Old friends ain't never gonna die.

12

FAMILY

*Unless the L*ᴏʀᴅ *builds the house,*
  its builders labor in vain.
*Unless the L*ᴏʀᴅ *watches over the city,*
  the watchmen stand guard in vain.
In vain you rise early
  and stay up late,
toiling for food to eat—
  for he grants sleep to those he loves.

*Sons are a heritage from the L*ᴏʀᴅ,
  children a reward from him.
Like arrows in the hands of a warrior
  are sons born in one's youth.
Blessed is the man
  whose quiver is full of them.
They will not be put to shame
  when they contend with their enemies in the gate.

Psalm 127

Many of the mighty man's greatest battles, victories and defeats will occur in his own household, because it is there that a man's character is most certainly tested and forged. It is with those whom we live every day that we reveal who we really are. We cannot hide at home. There, our true character, nature and influence is shown for good or ill. It is our wives, our children or our roommates who perceive us as no others do.

Our household will be the platform upon which our life is built, or it will be the destructive force which tears it down. We cannot think, "I need to do great things with my life right now. My family will have to wait until I get them done." Nor can we think, "It does not matter about my wife and kids. They will be okay. I need to do this other stuff, and they will still be here when it is all done." Such thinking is selfish, for while your personal dreams and goals are voluntary, your family obligations are not. You are the only husband of your wife; you are the only father of your children. No one can or should replace you in these responsibilities, and if you fail in them, who will be there to pick up the pieces?

If you need further persuasion, look at the examples of some of the men in the Bible who failed at home. Through these stories God gives us a solemn warning: "Do not go where these men have gone! Build a great marriage and home!" Consider Eli the prophet whose sons were sexually immoral and thieving. The word of God came to him saying that since he did not discipline his sons, they would die, and that the priesthood would be removed from his family. Consider Samuel, whose sons did not walk in his ways, and thus opened the door for the people of Israel to ask for a king—King Saul. Consider David, whose own example of adultery, deceit and murder was repeated one hundredfold by his children.

If these are not enough, look around you; look at your own relatives; look at the people in your own neighborhood; look even at the people in your church who have neglected what God has said about their marriages and families—look and be sobered. Look and see where you will end up if you do not build your family with love, hard work and spiritual principles.

I have a brief message for the single men: Prepare yourself for marriage. Very few men in this world are destined to live out their entire lives as single men. Too many of you are waiting too long to get married. The Bible teaches that it is better to marry than to struggle with lust. Many of the single men I know who have waited until late in their twenties (or longer!) to be married have paid a price of loneliness, immaturity and sexual frustration. Grow up; learn how to love a woman; then find her and marry her! Some of you may be afraid to marry because of what you saw in your own home as you grew up. Others of you may have experienced the heartbreak of divorce yourself. Do not allow what happened in your past or what you saw in people outside of God's kingdom to discourage you. God has a great plan. His plan for marriage is working for men all around you and will work for you as well!

Second Only to God

Next to your relationship to God, your family requires your greatest efforts in life. Your job is not next after God. Your sports are not next. Your yard, house, car and boat are not next. Not even your extra projects for the church are next. Next to God, you are to be most devoted to your wife, then your children. You must know this, and *they must know this.*

Prioritizing

Give your family a high priority in your time, efforts, thought and prayer. It will take immense effort to build a great marriage and family. Not that it is unpleasant or burdensome, but it simply will take the very best we have to give. It will not happen as a matter of course. If some of us worked as hard at our family life as we do our jobs, we would have amazing families! But our wives and kids are getting the leftovers—and it shows.

Loving

Become best friends with your wife. Be a team with her. Listen to her. Seek her advice and respect it. Spend time alone with her on a regular basis to talk, to plan, to share your hearts with one another. As I see it, men go to one extreme or the other: they are domineering and bossy with their wives, or they are weak and passive. We should balance the role of loving service with leadership.

Nurturing

Nurture and train your children. "Nurture" means that we love, encourage, listen to, play with and help our kids. "Train" means that we teach them to obey us, to obey and respect God, and that we teach them the principles of the Bible and how to live them out in their lives. Once again, we tend to go to extremes. We are either a nurturer who does not firmly discipline, or we are an authoritarian who is not close to his kids. A mighty man of God is both. He is mighty in giving love and affection, and he is powerful in administering discipline.

Serving

Be a servant in your home. I speak here of service of the most practical and menial kind. Keep your home in good repair. Perform the needed maintenance to keep things running well and looking good. Don't let the place get run down. Straighten up that garage or utility room! Keep your part of the closet neat and organized. Don't be slow to respond to your wife's requests for help—don't make her feel like she has to nag you to get you working around the house. If your wife lets you know something needs to be repaired, fix it yourself or call in someone who can. Remember that Solomon said, "If a man is lazy, the rafters sag; if his hands are idle, the house leaks" (Ecclesiastes 10:18). If your wife needs some extra help around the house, cheerfully pitch in. Don't be too proud to run the vacuum cleaner and do the dishes. Jesus was a servant—he washed feet and waited on tables. Do the same. Serve so eagerly and ably that the cleanliness and condition of your home gives glory to God!

Defining Success

Be more concerned for your family's spiritual growth than their worldly success. As mighty men, we want to excel. This is a godly impulse, but it is also one that becomes easily misguided. I am becoming increasingly alarmed at the drive for worldly success in many of our families. We want our kids to be at the top of their class, to be the best player on the team, to get the lead part in the play, to go to the elite schools, to be president of every club. When are we going to realize that our drive may be motivated by pride and that it could be putting immense pressure on our children? Certainly, we need to help our children discover and develop their talents. But the goal of life is not for them to be number one at everything. We claim it is for the glory of God, but is it really for *our* glory instead? I fear that some of us are going to pay a price of exasperated, bitter and worldly children who not only see through us, but who will one day walk away from the church. The answer is to train our kids to be spiritual, to love the kingdom first and to do their best. The rest will take care of itself.

Let me share a couple of stories that might help you.

A Daughter's Lesson

When our daughter Elizabeth entered into her senior year of high school, she had a dream of making the "top seven" (the varsity team) of her cross country team. She trained hard for months and was in the best shape of her life for the upcoming fall season. She went away on a project to help the poor with HOPE Worldwide that took her overseas. While there, she contracted some sort of intestinal malady that drained her of energy. She came back, ran her first race, collapsed at the finish line and was taken to the emergency room. She came through, but she was set back in her training. She was number eight on her team. As the time came for the state qualifying meet, one of the other girls was injured during the last few weeks of the season, and Elizabeth moved up to take her place. Her dreams had come true! She was going to get to go to the state meet after all!

Then one day her coach approached her to let her know the other girl had recovered from her injury and that she would be fit to run in the state competition. He said, "Elizabeth, you have worked hard, and if you want to run in the state meet, I won't stand in your way." Elizabeth knew what was best for her team (the other girl was faster than she), and she knew what she wanted for herself. She struggled and prayed over the decision and told her coach that she would step aside to make room for her teammate. Her coach, the other girl, the other parents—all were amazed. Several of them approached Elizabeth with tears in their eyes, saying they had never seen someone take such an unselfish step on behalf of the team.

To this day, when Elizabeth returns to high school meets to see her brothers run, someone usually comments to her about the decision she made. She won greater respect by stepping aside than by pushing her way forward. Our family was proud of her, and I, as her father, am more proud of her for that decision than if she had been the number one runner on her team. These are the kinds of decisions and moments that make a child, and a family, a spiritual or worldly one.

A Dad's Lesson

The second story is also about cross country. But this time it was me who had to learn the lesson. My son David easily made the "top seven." As the season progressed, David felt, as did his coach, that he was capable of running better times than he was turning in. David tried in every way he and his coach knew how, but he just never seemed to be able to break out and become the elite runner that he thought he could. I found myself getting more and more frustrated. I just knew David could make it! It began to affect me, and to affect my relationship with David.

Finally, I called my friend and discipler Steve Sapp and asked his advice. He told me that high school sports were meant to be fun and were a way for a kid to make friends, develop character and reach out to others. He advised me to lighten up and back off. I swallowed hard and took his advice. Did David go on to have the breakthrough race? No. He had a good season but not a great one.

But here is what happened shortly afterwards: David was also enrolled in a speech class that involved him in "Mock Trial," a contest that allows kids to get involved in simulated courtroom situations. With no experience and seemingly little effort, David quickly rose to the forefront of the class. He won "Best Attorney" and "Best Witness" at the regional competition. In the meantime, he kept up his straight A average and landed the leading male part in his high school's production of *West*

Side Story. Shortly after the play was over, he won a statewide oratorical contest for the Sons of the American Revolution and with it an all expense paid trip to compete in the national competition in San Diego, California.

What is the point? Our kids are going to do well in some areas, and in others they may not. As parents, we must encourage, support and help them. But we must guard against worldly motives and keep our own pride out of the picture—and we must not pressure them.

As a father trying to develop the talents and abilities of your kids, focus on character, effort, attitude and honesty. The rest will take care of itself!

An Inspiring Example

Mitch Mitchell, my coworker and friend on the staff at the Triangle Church, has worked as hard as any man I know to transform his marriage and family life. Several years ago, Mitch felt distant from his wife and was suffering a similar separation from his children. He was faithful to Jan and loved her dearly, but did not know how to express his feelings and was not powerfully leading the marriage. In a similar manner, he loved his children but was not deeply connected to them on an emotional or spiritual level. He especially felt this in his relationship with his son Josh. In working with Mitch, Geri and I gave him some simple advice: Be spiritual, give your family lots of time, and be a strong, godly leader. Mitch took on these challenges with a tremendous heart of humility, love and determination.

Over the last six years, the transformation in him, his wife and his children has been nothing short of amazing! Jan is a radiant, joyful wife who now works beside Mitch as his partner and best friend. Mitch is much closer to both of his children, and during the last few years, both of them have been baptized as disciples. Mitch's story is one of a man taking the challenge to love and lead his family and of a man determined to do whatever it would take to build a family life that would honor God. He has done it and has earned the love and respect not only of his wife and children, but of the entire Triangle Church because of it.

Let Mitch's story inspire you to believe that you, too, can see tremendous changes in your marriage and family. Family and marriage are the crucial proving ground of manhood.

Do not fail at home. Devote yourself to your wife and your children. The joy you will have because of them is unparalleled. A happy, godly wife, and children who turn out to be disciples are some of life's most precious victories. May God enable you to attain them! Be a mighty man at home. It will take a decision, devotion and determination, but it will pay dividends beyond compare for the rest of your life!

13

PROFESSION

Whatever you do, work at it with all your heart, as working for the Lord, not for men, since you know that you will receive an inheritance from the Lord as a reward. It is the Lord Christ you are serving.

Colossians 3:23-24

Our jobs give us a tremendous opportunity to bring glory to God and do mighty deeds. We should regard our work as a place and occasion to serve God, not simply a place to make a living and bide our time. Unfortunately, for many men work is a drudgery and a necessary evil. But for the Christian who understands God's sovereignty over all of life, work is much more than that.

Created to Work

When God created Adam and Eve, he gave them work to do: "The LORD God took the man and put him in the Garden of Eden to work it and take care of it" (Genesis 2:15). We are created by God with the innate compulsion to work, accomplish, achieve and create. Work and the desire within us to work are more than an instinct for survival; they are a vital part of what gives our lives purpose and meaning. They are a reflection of the image of God within us.

As he created, God would say, "It is good." Because we are made in God's image, there is something inside us that also longs to step back, look at our work and say, "It is good." We enjoy seeing the results of our labors. It gives us a sense of accomplishment, a sense of satisfaction. Even when we were children, we would rush home with our schoolwork or our art projects, show them to our parents and wait for their smiles and words of approval. As adults, we are the same way. Some of us have quenched this impulse, but it is still there. A man who will not work, who dislikes work or who forever complains about having to work, is fighting against his true nature. Even if we do not prefer our present work situation, we still need the feeling of accomplishment and fulfillment that work alone provides us.

Our work, then, should be a great and rewarding part of our lives. We should work with the goals of accomplishing something worthwhile and bringing glory to God. We should see beyond the humdrum to view a greater purpose for our work. If we are one of a thousand workers on an assembly line, we should value our job, and do it with a godly pride—we are a part of creating a needed product, something that betters the lives of people. If we are garbage collectors, we should envision ourselves as the men who keep our communities clean and beautiful. If we sell goods, we must see ourselves as providing people with something they need and do so in a way that makes them happy they did business with us. If we teach, we are not merely imparting facts, we are giving knowledge, changing lives, battling ignorance and giving our students better lives. If we are in health care, we are relieving sufferings and saving lives. Whatever our job, we must see beyond the surface. Only then will we be able to joyfully give our hearts to our work, seeing it as serving a greater purpose than merely providing us with a livelihood.

Excelling

We should strive for excellence in our work. We should strive to do the best we can, no matter what our job is. When God finished his work, he stood back and said, "It is good." Do you feel that way about your efforts? Do you feel you are doing your job well? If you are not, then you are undermining your manhood every day you go to work. "But my boss is unfair," you say, "and no one appreciates me or gives me credit for what I do." This is precisely why you should work for the glory of God, not for the praise of men. If God told Christian slaves in the early church to work enthusiastically even for harsh, uncaring masters because they were really working for him, then you can handle working for your boss!

Improving

We should strive to get better at what we do. Improve your skills. "Do you see a man skilled in his work? He will serve before kings; he will not serve before obscure men" (Proverbs 22:29). Get better at your job! Take extra classes. Read up on your field. Work on the physical, organizational, social and mental skills you need. Be like Joseph, who as both a slave and a prisoner, was so diligent and conscientious that he rose to the top. He was eventually rewarded by God for his diligence and faithfulness when Pharaoh discovered his talents and promoted him to be his prime minister!

"But they are holding me back," you say, "and no matter what I do, I don't get noticed or promoted." This may be true, but if you improve yourself, you will become a better person, no matter who notices! God will always notice, and you will respect yourself more when you see yourself getting better at what you do. I don't know if anyone encouraged those mighty men of David's army to learn to shoot their bows and sling their stones right- *and* left-handed, but they learned anyway (1 Chronicles 12:2). Quite a skill—even got them mentioned in the Bible! When was the last time you really took on something and got better at it?

As a preacher and minister, I am always striving to improve at what I do. I remember as a young man listening to tapes of great speakers like Winston Churchhill, Martin Luther King and Douglas MacArthur every morning as I prepared to leave for the office. In the early years of my ministry, I read book after book that helped me better understand the Bible. Commentaries, dictionaries—you name it—I devoured them (and still do) so that I could be a better teacher and preacher.

In the early years of my ministry, I led countless small group Bible discussions in which my rather pathetic speaking skills (and voice) were developed so that I could one day speak to thousands. I read books on speaking and training the voice so that I could improve the quality of my intonation. I developed the habit of recording any word I didn't know, looking it up, writing down the definition on a card and memorizing it. Why? Because I am a communicator and deal in words as a part of my job! One summer, I enrolled in a class in New Testament Greek. The class crammed one year of language study into eight intense weeks. It was difficult, but I loved it! I have continued to read books in my field (history) long after I graduated from college, just because I want to bring more knowledge to my speaking. I did all this and more to improve myself as a practitioner of ministry.

My whole writing career began in my mind and heart as a dream, a dream that I could help people by writing books. It has meant working harder and learning new skills, but it has been more than worth the effort. I have forced myself into the computer age. It has been challenging, but I am learning to use a voice dictation system as I write this book. I have not mastered it, but I am on the way! I have come a long way from the little word processor that looked like a microwave oven that I used when I wrote *Raising Awesome Kids in Troubled Times* a few years ago!

As we learn, we become more interested in our work. As we become better at what we do, we enjoy it more. We also gain self-respect and earn the respect of others who work with us. I challenge you, as a man and as a disciple: Keep learning; get better; grow in your job!

Getting Input

If you think you are in the wrong field, get some help. We have created an informal job evaluation group in the Triangle Church to help men get into the right profession and to help them become better established in the field they are in currently. George Hill, a podiatrist in our church (and one of the Mighty Men), recently began his own practice. He is an excellent physician, but the business side of medicine was not his métier (I told you I like learning new words!). I suggested that he get advice from several other of the Mighty Men who had business expertise and who had some knowledge of medicine. Since consulting with these brothers, and especially due to the professional help of Bill Thompson (also a physician, but who has earned his MBA so that he might work in the business side of health care), George has turned his practice around. He is on his way to paying off his college loans and is earning a place of respect in our community.

Other men have done the same. The point is this: it is foolish and wasteful for men to remain stuck in jobs with attitudes that hold them back. If a man will open up his life to the counsel of others, if he will seek to be the best he can be for God, then he can turn his work situation from a curse into a blessing!

The Joseph Project

Our Mighty Men in Triangle recently started a program we call "The Joseph Project." I came up with this idea one day while talking to the minister in charge of our singles group. Upon asking him what the singles most needed, he replied, "They need to get a life." As I further inquired what he meant, I found out that many of these young men were underemployed or were not trained for productive careers. Others were stuck in dead-end jobs or were working in fields for which they were not trained. I decided to put the Mighty Men to work on this. It entailed three Mighty Men meeting with three of our single men and then coming up with a plan to help each young man become a "Joseph," a young man who rises up from difficulty into greatness! Each of those Mighty Men would then mentor his "Joseph" for about six months through his ascent from mediocrity.

The program is still in its early stages, but we have already seen great results. We will start another group when this one is finished. Imagine the results in these young men's lives! Imagine the influence they will have, the marriages and families they will build, the dreams they will accomplish, and the godly impact they will have in our community—all because they learned how to get out of a dead end and start working for the glory of God!

A Victory Story

Dr. Estrada Bernard is one of the most respected members of our congregation and is a brilliant neurosurgeon who serves on the faculty at University of North Carolina. When Geri and I moved to the Triangle Church, Estrada's wife Cora, who is also a physician, was not a disciple. Estrada had a very demanding schedule and did not see Cora very often, and when he did, he was so exhausted that it was hard to build a close marriage. We worked diligently with Estrada to help him responsibly reduce his hours and run a more disciplined schedule. We also worked with him to help him become a more giving, loving husband.

In the meantime, Estrada became so frustrated with his work situation that when he was offered a position in another community with a considerable salary increase and better working hours, he was sorely tempted to take it. It would have meant, though, moving to a community a good distance away from the nearest church. I met with him several times and urged him not to take the position that was offered, but to take steps to make the best of his current situation. I pointed out to him that Cora would never be able to become a disciple if they moved away, and that his newborn son, E. J., would not have the opportunity to be raised in a church that would teach him to become a disciple.

Estrada decided to make the best of it: to buckle down, work smarter and work as best he could under a difficult supervisor. During the next few months, his supervisor decided to take the job that Estrada turned down. It was also during this time that Cora decided to become a disciple. Estrada was then offered the position his boss had vacated. He took the new job and is now the Chief of Neurosurgery at UNC Hospital. He has a beautiful Christian wife and a young son who is growing up learning to love God! If we put God first in our jobs, even though our situation may become difficult at times, God will bring about something better for us!

Your working situation may not be all you wish it was, but do not let that stop you! As a mighty man of God, determine that you will rise above the situation. Decide that you will look beyond the daily grind to see the plan of God. Resolve that you will strive for excellence, that you will improve yourself, and that you will seek God's kingdom first, no matter what. Then sit back, be patient and watch what God will do!

14

BENEVOLENCE

A generous man will prosper;
he who refreshes others will himself be refreshed.

Proverbs 11:25

A mighty man is a generous man with an open heart and an open hand. He is powerful in good deeds; he is strong in helping the weak, the poor and those in need. A benevolent man sees a need and immediately springs into action. Is someone sick? Is someone in financial distress? Is someone in trouble? The mighty man is their defender and their helper; he is the gallant knight who comes to the rescue!

Biblical Illustrations

It was said of the young Jerusalem church that "there were no needy persons among them" (Acts 4:34). This was because people shared what they had. When their brothers did not have enough, they shared their possessions with them. What would move people to do such a thing? The example of Jesus was certainly a powerful incentive, but they had a living example as well: Joseph, the Levite from Cyprus.

The Bible tells us that it was this man who, in the early days of the church, sold his property to help his needy brothers (Acts 4:36-37). Because of his benevolent example, others joined in. He was so loving and giving that the apostles gave him the name Barnabas, which means "Son of Encouragement" (Acts 4:36). What an incredible man, and what a great influence in the history of God's church! He was a mighty man, powerful in his generosity.

Would you be a mighty man? Become a bighearted, generous man.

Some men have the gift of making money. Everything they touch turns a profit. They are wise businessmen with an instinct and a mind for finances. If you are such a man, then use your gift to make a great amount of money—and then give it away! So many problems could be helped or solved if more men were generous in this way. People need spiritual help, they need wisdom, they certainly need prayer, but sometimes what they really need is cold, hard cash! We need the financial resources to preach the gospel around the world, and we also need money to help relieve the sufferings of the poor and the sick and to meet the needs of our own members who are in distress.

Modern Day Examples
Giving Financially

Art Belden is a man known for his benevolence in the Triangle Church. Art and his wife, Diane, were converted just a few years ago. When they came to the church, their marriage was on the rocks, their children were unhappy and they were beset with severe personal struggles. They saw that God was the answer for their problems and were soon baptized into Christ. They were and still remain very grateful to God for saving their lives and souls.

Art has a job of significant responsibility and influence. He is well compensated for his efforts and lives in a nice home, but he realizes that all of his affluence would have been for naught had not he and his wife become disciples. Art and Diane have gladly committed themselves to being generous. Without fanfare and without being asked, they continually help those in need. They do far more good than any one of us knows. The Beldens are not only generous with their resources, but are two of the most hospitable and evangelistic members of our congregation. It is obvious to all who know him that the more Art gives away, the more God blesses him. This modern day Barnabas is a beloved mighty man who has helped and inspired many in our church.

Giving Expertise

Rick Overturf is the kind of man who knows how things work. He can exorcise the demons from any malfunctioning mechanical contraption on the planet! When Rick was challenged to be a Mighty Man in the Triangle Church, he decided to put his abilities to work, and he did so in an ingenious way. He observed that many of the single mothers in our church had cars that were badly in need of repair.

Rick planned to fix the cars, but he wanted to accomplish more than that. He decided to train a group of men in the fine art of basic auto maintenance. He gathered together about ten willing men from our church and identified a group of the single moms whose cars needed work. Then one Saturday he set up a car repair shop in the church parking lot. I will never forget the sight as I drove in that day. There were cars everywhere—hoods open, engines running (or attempting to run!) and large numbers of men leaning over and crawling under cars. And there was Rick, running from car to car giving advice and overseeing the whole thing. Off to the side stood a group of women smiling, laughing, watching their kids and waiting for their cars to be fixed up—for free! All they had to do was supply the parts. It was one of the happiest sights I had seen in many a day and a proud moment for me as I saw Rick and all the brothers helping out the sisters. I thought, *This is the way God's church is supposed to be!* and I thanked God for Rick and his team of mechanics.

Rick figures he has done over $17,000 in repairs already, and he's just getting started! He has also taught some brothers some needed skills and, more importantly, has taught them to care about and serve those in need.

What can you do to help the needy? What is out there waiting for you to do? Take it on. You may have money to give—

then give it. You may have the skill to fix a single woman's car or repair her home or to paint a widow's house. You may want to mow a yard, give a ride, whatever—do it! We need a new order of knighthood to arise in our churches. We need thousands of men who will be mighty in benevolence.

As we do so, not only will we make a tremendous difference in our churches and communities, but we ourselves will live under God's blessing because "blessed is he who is kind to the needy" (Proverbs 14:21).

15

FRUITFULNESS

It is God who arms me with strength
and makes my way perfect.
He makes my feet like the feet of a deer;
he enables me to stand on the heights.
He trains my hands for battle;
my arms can bend a bow of bronze.
You give me your shield of victory,
and your right hand sustains me;
you stoop down to make me great.

Psalm 18:32-35

We are at war. We are in a conflict far more significant than any battle David's mighty men ever fought. At stake is not earthly territory or money or power or wealth or any of the other things for which the countless wars of history have been waged. We are in a battle for the souls of men. We are seeking to win men and women away from their allegiance to this world and bring them to heaven. Every disciple is a soldier in this war, and every one of us must do our part, as Paul taught:

For though we live in the world, we do not wage war as the world does.
The weapons we fight with are not the weapons of the world. On the
contrary, they have divine power to demolish strongholds. We demolish
arguments and every pretension that sets itself up against the knowl-
edge of God, and we take captive every thought to make it obedient to
Christ. (2 Corinthians 10:3-5)

The Warrior Spirit

If we are to win this war, we must awaken the warrior spirit within the men of God's kingdom. For too long the men of the church have been complacent while the battle raged around them. It is time we woke up. It is time that we put on our armor, took up our shields, grasped our swords, and went forth to do battle.

It will take courage. It has always taken courage to reach out to people, to share our faith with them. We risk being misunderstood, rejected, criticized and persecuted. But there is no other way.

Paul said that he was willing to become all things to all men that he might save souls. How about you? What are you willing to change so that you will become more effective in bearing evangelistic fruit for the Lord? Many of us have not led anyone else to Christ in months or years. What is the reason? Is it that we have become cowardly and timid, afraid to reach out, afraid to say the things that people need to hear? No one comes into the kingdom unless someone has the boldness to invite them and then to present them the truth of God's word. Are there more women than men being brought into the kingdom today because our sisters are more courageous than we?

Weapons of Love

Our weapons are no longer the weapons of violence but of love. We are not out to destroy other people but to win them to Jesus. They are not the enemy; Satan is. He is the one in opposition to us, not them. We must have a heart of love that goes out in compassion to those who are lost in sin. Only when others see the depth of our love will they listen to our words.

I want to challenge you as a man and a brother to awaken within you the spirit of the warrior and get into the fight to win others to Jesus. I especially want to encourage you to reach out to other men. Too long have the sisters led the way in converting other women. When we read the story of the early church in the book of Acts, we sense that the numbers of men grew just as rapidly as did the numbers of women. Sadly, it is not that way today. The reason is not because men in our time are less open; it is because the brothers in today's church are not as bold.

One of the primary reasons that we are not fruitful is because we are not respected by men of the world. We have not become mighty men, and it shows in our inability to evangelize other men. It especially shows in our failure to convert more men of strong character. Men outside of God's kingdom are looking for men worthy of respect, men that they can confidently follow. If they see in our lives the qualities of manhood exemplified by Jesus and the great heroes of the Bible, they will be much more likely to listen to us as we share our faith with them. But if they see in our lives a lack of masculinity, a weak character or a mediocre example, they will not give ear to our message. It is only when the men of God's kingdom rise up and become true mighty men that we will see the floodgates open and large numbers of men become disciples.

It is time to pick up the sword of the Spirit and go into battle. It is time to go out on a mission far more important than those of David's mighty men. It is time to obey our commanding officer who said, "Go and make disciples of all nations" (Matthew 28:19). This was Jesus' final earthly command to his church, and it is still his great purpose for his kingdom today. This was the preoccupation of his mind, heart and life, and it is what he wants his disciples to be all about now.

You need to become a warrior again. You need to once again smell the smoke of the battle and hear the cries of the wounded. You need to strive in the battle with such energy that you fall exhausted at the end of the day with your hand frozen to the sword. You need to feel once again in your soul the satisfaction of knowing you have been courageous, that you have done your best, that you have given your all. You need to once again experience the thrill and exaltation of victory, the victory of a soul saved and a man's life redeemed.

Then you will fulfill the purpose for which Jesus brought you into his army: that you might go forth to battle as a soldier, fight the good fight and come home to rest one day, receiving your crown of glory.

Then you will know what it really means to be a mighty man of God!

16

FITNESS

You, O LORD, keep my lamp burning;
my God turns my darkness into light.
With your help I can advance against a troop;
with my God I can scale a wall.

Psalm 18:28-29

The heroes of the Bible were virile, dynamic and active. They strike me as physically energetic and strong. From Moses to Joshua to Samuel to David to Elijah to John the Baptist to Peter, James and John and certainly to Jesus, the men of the Bible were physically dynamic men.

God created us as beings of spirit and body, and as men, we dare not neglect the nurture of either one. Our body is the temple of the Holy Spirit. Even a cursory knowledge of the tabernacle in the time of Moses and the temple Solomon built tells us that these were splendid, magnificent and beautiful structures that reflected the beauty and glory of God. Now that we are privileged to be the dwelling place of the Spirit of God on earth, how dare we think we can neglect our bodies?

The Problem

I am saddened and sickened by the physical decrepitude I observe in the men around me, even many in God's kingdom. This is shameful, is a sin against God, and is an affront to him who made us in his image. We must radically repent.

We cannot separate how we are doing spiritually from how we are doing physically. The Bible teaches that our bodies are the temples of the Holy Spirit (1 Corinthians 6:19). The two are irrevocably joined together. When we neglect our bodies or abuse them, when we allow our health to deteriorate, it has a direct impact on our spiritual growth and our closeness to God. A man who overeats, smokes, abuses alcohol or drugs, or in any other way neglects or destroys his own body is sinning against God. A man who allows his body to become soft and weak is limiting his effectiveness, influence and vitality in his service to God. Such a man is also losing respect among other men, his children and his wife.

I have often found that taking on a new physical challenge was the precursor to a time of significant spiritual growth in my life. When we are disciplined in our habits and energetic in our activities, it spills over and benefits our spiritual progress. Our minds are enlivened, our mood is elevated, our anxiety diminishes, and our dreams are reawakened. We find we are able to accomplish much more in a day than we were before. Our decision making becomes crisper, sharper and quicker. We sleep better and awaken feeling energetic and ready to tackle the tasks of the day.

But when we have neglected and abused our bodies, illness sets in. We become sickly and lethargic: the challenges of life weigh heavier upon us, and stress rules in our hearts. We are not as happy, cheerful and optimistic as we should be.

No Excuses

I can hear the excuses coming: "But I am too busy! My job, family and church obligations do not allow me to get any exercise." "I am getting older, and you just have to accept that you're going to slow down and put on some weight when you get to my age." "I'm just not the athletic type. I'm not drawn to sports and physical activity." "Well, the old high school knee injury is acting up. And ever since I strained my back a few months ago, I just haven't been the same." "I'm more concerned about growing spiritually that I am about being some macho sports freak." "As soon as I get out of school, I'll do something." "As soon as my schedule lightens up, I'll get a plan." "As soon as the kids' soccer season is over, I'll make the time to work out." Heard enough?

For those of you making these excuses, let me give you a couple of others that might be coming your way soon: "As soon as I get out of this hospital bed..."; or "as soon as my divorce is settled...." Am I being an alarmist? Am I overreacting? I don't think so. But I do know this: If you keep on making the same old excuses that most men make, your health is just going to keep going downhill and with it, your manhood.

Inspiration

Let's look at a couple of Biblical examples. Consider Moses, who died when he was 120 years old and of whom it was said that "his eyes were not weak nor his strength gone" (Deuteronomy 34:7), or consider Caleb. This eighty-five-year-old man's example is so powerful that we will just let his own words speak for him:

> "So here I am today, eighty-five years old! I am still as strong today as the day Moses sent me out; I'm just as vigorous to go out to battle now as I was then. Now give me this hill country that the LORD promised me that day. You yourself heard then that the Anakites were there and their cities were large and fortified, but, the LORD helping me, I will drive them out just as he said." (Joshua 14:10-12)

What an amazing man! Here is a real man's man, a man we can look up to and admire. You can feel the energy pouring out of him 3,000 years later! I don't know about you, but when I turn eighty-five, I hope I am as fired up and energetic as this guy!

Men, why you do think all these examples are in the Bible? *They are there to inspire and instruct you on how to be a man.* The fact is, many of us have surrendered our masculinity and are living our lives as physical, emotional and spiritual weaklings. Aren't you tired of living this way? Aren't you tired of looking at yourself in the mirror and being disgusted at what you see? Aren't you tired of your wife dropping hints that you should go to the gym more and get some exercise? Aren't you tired of being exhausted all the time? Aren't you tired of catching every cold that comes through town? Aren't you tired of wishing your wife was more attracted to you, that you felt better about yourself sexually and that your love life was more exciting? I want to urge you with everything I have within me to make a decision this day that you are going to get in shape and stay in shape for the rest of your life!

The Practicals

Consistent

Decide what you are going to do to get in shape, and be consistent with it. Any physical activity done consistently is helpful—walking, running, biking, weight training—as long as we do it and do it consistently every week.

Aerobic

Do something aerobic—get your heart rate up—several times a week. If you have been out of shape, walking is a great way to start. I would add, however, that walking is not going to be enough for most of us. You are going to need to run, ride a bicycle or stationary bike, or do something more vigorous if you're really going to get in good shape. As I am out running, I see quite a few overweight walkers and very few obese runners. I am not trying to discourage you if you are just getting started (because you should not go out and try to run long distances if you are overweight); but my point is, speed up that walking into running, and you will get lean!

Strength Training

Do something to increase your muscular strength. When a man is physically strong, it makes him more masculine. Strength makes him feel better about himself. It also makes his wife much more attracted to him! What I first started weight training, my wife said, "You don't need to get any bigger. You look just fine the way you are." As I began to get some results and get stronger, she changed her tune: "Oo-oo! You look good!" The minute I heard that, I ran to the gym, hit a new one-rep max on the bench press, and dedicated myself to weight training for the rest of my life! Seriously, increasing our muscular strength helps us to avoid many of the injuries that debilitate us as we age: backache, headache, muscle pulls and strains. Lean muscle also burns more calories and burns them faster. An increasing body of research supports the notion that to be truly healthy, we need to be more than aerobically fit, we need to be physically stronger as well.

Trim Down

Get leaner. Obese, pudgy men are not masculine men. Get rid of the fat! Many of us have embarked upon exotic diets to no avail. For most of us the solution is simple: *Burn up more than you're putting in!* This means that we need to reduce the calories coming in and use up more through exercise. If you do this, you *will* lose weight! A reasonable diet in which we cut back on fatty foods, sugary desserts and junk food (especially those eaten later in the evening) will probably produce in most of us some very encouraging results. You may have to enlist some brothers to hold you accountable, and your wife to help get the kitchen purged of your lifetime supply of Twinkies, but it can be done! In all my years of working with people, I have made a simple discovery: *No one loses weight unless they decide to do it themselves.* I urge you, for the sake of your health, your influence, your self-esteem, your marriage and your manhood—get leaner!

Get Outdoors

Most of the men of the Bible spent a great deal of their time outdoors. They were men of the open air, of the desert, of the sea and of the woodlands. Jesus walked most places he went. When he was not walking, he was sailing under the open sky. David lived in the desert for years, as did Moses and Abraham. It seems to me that when Lot moved from the outdoors into Sodom, and David moved from the desert into Jerusalem, their troubles began. Jesus often came into the towns and villages, but then would retreat to the outdoors to be alone with God.* A man who spends time outdoors is more ener-

*I refer you to chapter 4 of my book *Be Still, My Soul* for a full discussion of this important topic (Woburn, Mass.: Discipleship Publications International, 1998).

getic, more healthy, more relaxed, more in tune with God and for lack of a better word, more normal. Get up, get out of the house, and get outside!

Play Time

Select a sport you enjoy and participate regularly in it. Not only do we need exercise, but we need to play. Find a sport (or sports) you really enjoy doing and get into it! You may prefer a team sport like basketball or flag football. You might select an outdoor sport like biking, hiking, camping, sailing or mountain climbing. The only rule is, you must enjoy it. We need time away from our routines to recreate ourselves. We need to go out, have fun and get our minds completely off the serious business that has occupied us during the week. One of the best ways to do this is by playing. Many of us have become dull, boring and lifeless as men *because we don't play anymore.* We need to regain our childlike hearts! It will make us more useful and happier men. It will teach us not to take ourselves so seriously. Whenever I come back home after a morning playing flag football with the guys at church, I find myself relaxed, fired up and ready to take on whatever is ahead of me. And, at forty-nine years old, I am glad that I can still compete with (and defeat!) the younger guys.

Many of the men in our congregation have taken up camping. They enjoy going out alone or with other friends, and they enjoy taking their families. What a great, inexpensive way to get away and to spend time with our families! It draws families together by getting them out into God's creation and teaching them to work as a team.

It is my fervent prayer that many of you will realize the seriousness of your situation and make a decision to become physically fit. I hope that you will not dismiss what I have said, but will realize the godly, spiritual reasons behind it. I hope that many of you will, after reading this chapter, resolve to become a true mighty man of physical strength, stamina and vitality!

17

A Man Past Forty

"I am still as strong today as the day Moses sent me out; I'm just as vigorous to go out to battle now as I was then."

Joshua 14:11

The age of forty is universally regarded as a crucial turning point in a man's life. Some dread it, others ignore it, many joke about it, and few celebrate it. In a culture and age that glorifies youth and beauty, aging is the ultimate and final defeat. For many, age forty marks the beginning of the end, the slow decline into senility, decrepitude and oblivion, the autumn years that await the icy fingers of a winter's death. Life is no longer to be lived with manly verve and vitality—those times are gone forever, the domain of our former selves and of younger men. Ours is but to hang on in obscurity and resignation to an increasingly diminishing role and impact.

How different from this bleak portrayal is the bright and glorious picture painted for us by the mind of God! As we read the Bible, we see that maturity is to be prized and respected—even wished for. We see that one of the most dreaded signs of maturity—gray hair—rather than a badge of shame to be chemically concealed, is instead a crown of honor to be proudly displayed: "Gray hair is a crown of splendor; it is attained by a righteous life" (Proverbs 16:31). We see the promises that assure us of a deepening and ripening blessing in the last half of life, not abandonment by God to a life of "has-beenism."

But we must deal with the hard facts of reality as we see them in the lives of men around us. For most men, the forties and beyond are years to be dreaded for good reason. Having disobeyed or ignored God in the first half of life, they then reap the bitter harvest of the folly they have sown.

What is a man of God to do? How is he to look at his life after forty? We will consider the dangers and the opportunities of life after forty, and will conclude with some advice to help us in our quest. My hope is that no matter where you may be in your journey, you may live the last half of your life victoriously, as a mighty man of God.

The Dangers

One of the dangers of passing forty is that we surrender to physical decline. "But we are aging, aren't we? Isn't it better to graciously accept it, rather than fighting the inevitable?" If you mean by your question that we are to accept the fact that we no longer have the recuperative powers of youth, that we may need more rest, that we will get some wrinkles and that perhaps we will experience the graying or loss of our hair, I am with you heart and soul. It is a foolish thing for maturing men to try to dress like teens or retain the appearance of their senior high school annual portrait. Some men do, and the results are not flattering! I, for one, never want to return to the lacquered, helmet-haired, goofy look I had as a young guy. But when I say "surrender to physical decline," I have in mind something much more serious, sinful and prevalent.

What I mean is that many older men (and even some men in their twenties and thirties) have given up staying in shape. In the name of aging they laugh off or glibly dismiss their pudgy waistlines and puffy faces with a "Well, I'm just getting older," kind of attitude. Their wives and children roll their eyes in rueful acknowledgment of this man's self-deceived surrender to laziness, wishing that he would see the light, stop making such foolish excuses, and get in shape. We must see this attitude for what it is: a lie to ourselves, a dishonoring of God, a frustration to our wives and an embarrassment to our children.

Such men have not only surrendered to obesity, they have forfeited respect. The tragedy is that not only have they lost the respect of their loved ones and peers, but they have also lost self-respect.

Deep within ourselves, we all value fitness and want to be healthy and vibrant. We may be tired of trying, we may feel powerless before our appetites and weaknesses, but we wish for a toned, attractive and energetic body.

For a man to accept an early diminishing of vitality or loss of his health is often the first step toward a worse surrender: the signing away of his dreams, his drive and his love of life itself. By doing so, we cheat God of his plans to use us; we rob our wives of the vibrant men they married; we steal from our families precious years we could have shared with them. We could live long and healthy lives, but instead we foolishly throw years away as our failure to protect and enhance our health leads us into years of incapacity or to an early death.

Time's Up?

After we turn forty, many of us feel that our life direction and pattern is set, that it is too late to change. We say, "I'd better accept the way things are now, because that's the way it's going to be for the rest of my life." What a faithless, defeatist attitude! How it denies the promises of God and the example of so many great men! If we are not careful, this destructive mindset can subtly overtake us. The result? A defeated, dull, discouraged and dreamless man who is no fun to be around and who will live out his own dire self-prophecy.

Haunting Mistakes

Mistakes from our past can rise up to haunt us as we get older. The forties and beyond can be a time in which we reap the blessings of the good seed we have sown: our marriages, our children, our careers, our reputations, our friendships. The efforts we have made for years can come to fruition in this time, but the opposite is also true. The sins of our youth and young adulthood can come back to plague us. Particularly will they show up in our marriages and in our children. The sickly marriage we failed to nourish may finally be pronounced dead. The children we neglected, spoiled or pressured may rise up to curse us. The friendships we failed to build or neglected to nurture will not be there as our comfort in times of loneliness and defeat. Our financial wastefulness and lack of professional growth can result in our still not being in a solid career or in sound financial shape as the time approaches for our children to go to college or for us to retire.

Failing Faith

Cynicism, anger, discouragement and depression can set in after forty. Listen to these words of a man who looked at life with a sense of defeat and sorrow:

> So I hated life, because the work that is done under the sun was grievous to me. All of it is meaningless, a chasing after the wind. (Ecclesiastes 2:17)

As we get older, we start figuring out that life is hard and often unfair. Bad things happen to us. We lose a job because of someone's personal grudge or because we don't fit in with somebody's plan. We are let down, no, stabbed in the back, by people we thought were our friends. We see our spiritual heroes fall away from the faith. And perhaps most painful of all, we disappoint ourselves. We fail to live up to our own ideals and commitments. We see that we missed some opportunities because we failed to act quickly, or we believe that someone stepped in ahead of us and got the prize we thought was destined to be ours. We see that we have sinned and perhaps have sinned in ways that have altered the fabric of our lives forever. We think, *If only I had not done that,* or *If only I had done that differently.* Our days past forty can pass in slow and dreary procession as we unceasingly analyze and rehearse the "what-ifs" of life.

The result is anger. Anger at ourselves. Anger at someone else. Anger at the church. Anger at a leader. Anger at our wives, our children. Anger at everybody. Anger at life. Anger at God. Unresolved anger will lead to depression. Many men I know who are "down" are really just mad! They may not realize that they are angry, or they may not know at what or whom they are mad, but rarely have I known a depressed man who, deep inside his soul, was not an angry man.

Our anger shows in our sour and crabby demeanor. We become bitter old men—in our forties! We have a sneer, a leer and a jeer for everything. We don't know the laughter of joy anymore; we only know the snide snicker of the cynic. We have something critical, mocking and sarcastic to say to everybody about everything. We take the fun and joy right out of any occasion by our sullen, gloomy, cloudy and sulking spirit. We don't like to go to parties, have fun, play or smile; we are too busy being angry old men.

We feel there is no way out. We have lost our childlike faith that God can fix anything, that God is going to work out everything for our good. And so we mope in our sadness and gloom. We may continue to go to work, go to church, go through the motions of our marriage and family life, but the glory and joy have departed. We have no more high hopes, no more sparkling dreams and no more great expectations. We are dead men waiting for the undertaker.

Think Again

As a man who has stared these attitudes in the face, I utterly reject such nonsense! I reject it as a denial of the promises of God. I reject it as a ruination of my wife, children and friends and all I hold dear. I reject that it is as a waste of my life. I reject it as a waste of your life. I reject that it is an inevitable consequence of aging. I reject it as an affront to my manhood. And I reject it as an insult to Almighty God.

I urge you with everything within me to rise up and live out the true destiny of your manhood. Get up out of your laziness and despair, and live so gloriously that the brightness of your latter years drives the darkness from every corner of your life. Let the light of God so shine upon you that the days of darkness are forgotten and only recalled with the grateful knowledge that they are gone forever.

Think about the great men of the Bible. Men like Abraham who, at seventy-five years old, was called by God to get up, leave his homeland and go to a country he had never seen—a man who was promised that his descendants would outshine the stars of heaven! Men like Moses, who thought he was done for, who thought his murderous ways had forever ruined his life, who, at eighty, was called to go and lead God's people out of bondage into freedom. Think about Caleb, valiant, strong Caleb, who at age forty was consigned to wander in the desert with his rebellious, faithless brothers until they died off for sins he did not commit. Think about Caleb as an eighty-five-year-old man who is approached by Joshua as he prepares to lead the Israelites to cross the Jordan and conquer the promised land:

> *"So here I am today, eighty-five years old! I am still as strong today as the day Moses sent me out; I'm just as vigorous to go out to battle now as I was then. Now give me this hill country that the LORD promised me that day. You yourself heard then that the Anakites were there and their cities were large and fortified, but, the LORD helping me, I will drive them out just as he said."*
> *Then Joshua blessed Caleb son of Jephunneh and gave him Hebron as his inheritance. (Joshua 14:10-13)*

Think about Caleb! Think about men like Paul, who, as an older man, confined to a dank Roman jail, writes the most joyful letter in the Bible; Paul who, in spite of his critics within and without the church, says,

> *But what does it matter? The important thing is that in every way, whether from false motives or true, Christ is preached. And because of this I rejoice.*
> *Yes, and I will continue to rejoice....For to me, to live is Christ and to die is gain. (Philippians 1:18, 21)*

Think about him, and be encouraged! Think about him, and rise up again! Think about all these men, and do not spend another day in surrender to death and decay, but look forward to your life becoming more and more glorious—more zealous, more loving, more joyful and more like Jesus!

The Opportunities

Hard-Won Wisdom

Maturity means wisdom. Now that you have lived forty years, believe it or not, you have learned a few things! Let your maturity work for you, not against you. Let the lessons of dear-bought experience pay off in wiser decision making; don't repeat your mistakes. Become a wise and trusted advisor for younger people. Your experience is needed by others; don't let it go to waste. You may not be able to undo your mistakes, but you can help others not to make them.

Maturity means that our marriages should be getting better. By now we should know our wives very well. We should now know much more how to love, encourage and comfort them. Our sex lives should be getting better: more intense, more passionate, more exciting, more adventurous, more romantic, more thrilling. As I have often said, honeymoons are wasted on amateurs. As we get older, our sex life should get better because we understand one another better, are more in love, are more comfortable with each other, and are more intimate.

Our maturity should be paying off in our job performance. We should be so skilled that we are regarded as experts. We should be constantly improving. Who says we have to burn out and become outdated old relics as we get older? Try telling that to Paul, Moses and Peter! I am far better at what I do now than I was in my younger years. I know God better, and I know people better. I know the Bible better. I am a better speaker, better motivator, better organizer, better trainer and better teacher. I am a more fiery and zealous preacher now than I was ten or twenty years ago. What I used to know in theory, I now know for a fact. I believe in God's promises more than I used to because I've lived long enough to see them fulfilled over time. Like Joshua I can say,

> *"'... You know with all your heart and soul that not one of all the good promises the LORD your God gave you has failed. Every promise has been fulfilled; not one has failed.'" (Joshua 23:14)*

Never Too Late

You still can change things. Yes, you have made some mistakes, maybe some big ones. Some of those will have ongoing consequences for you, but that doesn't mean you have to be stuck where you are. Someone once said, "Don't let what you can't do keep you from doing what you can do." There is much you can still do. Paul could not bring back the lives he took as a persecutor of the church, but he could save as many as possible. Moses could not bring back the Egyptian he killed, but he could lead God's people to freedom. Peter could not unsay his fateful words, "I don't know the man!" but he could say some fifty days later, as he stood on trial before the highest court in the land, "Salvation is found in no one else"! Mark could not undo his weak-willed retreat from the mission field, but he could repent, write the gospel that bears his name, and change so powerfully that the apostle whom he disappointed could say years later, "Get Mark and bring him with you, because he is helpful to me in my ministry" (2 Timothy 4:11).

Once and for all, quit allowing your past to ruin your present, and start enjoying your life!

Some Advice

Let me close with some practical advice for those over forty, and for those approaching these great years.

Develop Spiritual Muscle

Keep on growing spiritually. Be like Paul, who wrote,

Not that I have already obtained all this, or have already been made perfect, but I press on to take hold of that for which Christ Jesus took hold of me. Brothers, I do not consider myself yet to have taken hold of it. But one thing I do: Forgetting what is behind and straining toward what is ahead, I press on toward the goal to win the prize for which God has called me heavenward in Christ Jesus. (Philippians 3:12-14)

Learn the Lessons

Don't repeat your mistakes. Learn from the mistakes of your past. One of the real failures I see in older men is the failure to learn from their past. God uses our mistakes to teach us, but he will have to keep hammering you on the same point until you get it. As I have often said, "Life consists of learning the lessons you should have already learned." Don't let this be true for you!

Share the Wealth

Share your wisdom with others. If God has put you through some trials, one reason is so that you might become effective in encouraging others who are going through those same trials (2 Corinthians 1:3-11). Many men I know have a gold mine of experience they could be sharing with those younger than they, yet they remain silent. This not only deprives younger people of the wisdom of age, it also deprives you of the increasing conviction that comes as you share what you know with others.

Fight the Good Fight

Fight physical, mental and spiritual decline. Don't take as a matter of course that your physical and mental powers are going to plummet as you get older. If you believe that, they surely will. Yes, aging is inevitable, but that does not mean we should assume that we are going to become decrepit and useless next month! Let God decide when to take you out—don't do it for him!

I would urge you to challenge your mind with learning. Memorize—scripture, poetry, whatever. Learn a language. Enroll in a class at night; it is a great way to meet people, is incredibly useful and will do much to keep you mentally fresh. Learn some new skills. Get into the computer age. Why don't some of us over-forty guys get jobs in places where we can help to start a new church?

Take on some other things that challenge you mentally and physically. Learn a skill. Take dance classes. Learn to repair your car. Take up a new sport. Go back to school and learn a new trade if you need to. All of these skills, hobbies and fun things don't have to be an exercise in selfishness—they can be dedicated to the glory of God and used to advance his kingdom.

My wife and I have both taken up new interests in recent years. Geri has always wanted to learn to play the piano, and now she's finally doing it! We bought her a piano and got her some lessons. She is loving it, and it is challenging her dexterity and mental sharpness and is stimulating her mind and emotions in a powerful way. I learned New Testament Greek in my mid-thirties and am going to begin reviewing those notes as soon as I finish this book. I plan to learn Hebrew, and I look up any English word I don't know, put it on a card and memorize it. I ran a marathon at the age of forty-eight. (And yes, I had knee surgery more than ten years earlier).

All of these things have added a tremendous amount of joy and satisfaction to our lives and have provided us with countless opportunities to share our faith with people we never would have met just sitting at home mourning our age.

Enjoy Life!

> Then I realized that it is good and proper for a man to eat and drink, and to find satisfaction in his toilsome labor under the sun during the few days of life God has given him—for this is his lot. Moreover, when God gives any man wealth and possessions, and enables him to enjoy them, to accept his lot and be happy in his work—this is a gift of God. He seldom reflects on the days of his life, because God keeps him occupied with gladness of heart. (Ecclesiastes 5:18-20; also read 9:7-10)

Solomon says we should enjoy life. He knew life could be hard and that we would have our moments of despair. He also knew that everything about life was not fair. But he determined that he was going to be happy anyway, because even though life presented many difficulties, there was still a loving and just God. Solomon urges us to be happy in the simple things. The longer I live, the more this advice makes sense. I have figured out that I don't need to waste any more time worrying about everything and everybody. I am not God. I can't fix everything. I will do what I can, and I will strive with all my might to speak up for God and for what is right. I will help everyone I can to find God and to stay faithful once they have, but I cannot live their lives for them. I cannot right every wrong either in the kingdom or in the world.

Jesus didn't try to right every wrong in his world. He preached the truth, and he lived by it. But he also really enjoyed life: he went to weddings; he loved his friends; he loved children; he spent lots of time outdoors, alone with God. He liked and loved people. He was a happy man. Isn't it about time we became happy, too?

It is my conviction that the forties can be the beginning of a wondrous time in our lives if we will so decide. They can be a time when, having been seasoned and weathered by life, we can face the rest of our days with wisdom and appreciation. They can be years when we take the time to become the person we never made time to be in our younger days. They should be a time when we fall even more deeply in love with our wives and begin watching our children blossom into maturity of their own. Even though all these things will not happen perfectly, we can decide to enjoy and embrace the life God has given us—difficulties, challenges, joys and all. But most importantly, no matter what may go on in our lives, the forties and beyond must be a time when we draw ever closer to our Father in heaven as children who love him, revere his Son, understand ourselves and relish life as never before.

And hey—if we have to ride off into the sunset, at least roar off on a Harley Davidson, mighty man sword in hand!

The Mightiest Man of Them All

Jesus is the mightiest man of all. Whatever we need to do, he has already accomplished. Whatever we need to become, he already is. He is both the goal of our lives and our inspiration, the challenge of our life and the source of our power. He is our perfect example, the man who possessed in full all the qualities of other Biblical heroes combined—but without sin.

He had the faith of Abraham; the righteousness, discipline and purity of Joseph; the passion, force, and self-surrender of Moses; the courage and charisma of Joshua; the pure and singing heart of David; the boldness and righteousness of the prophets; the joy and exuberance of Peter; the audacity, intellect and drive of Paul; the love of John...all these he had in full measure and without sin. He is the mightiest of them all!

To follow him, and to imitate his matchless and perfect life is the most noble and daunting task a man could ever assume. Some of you are already throwing up your hands in frustration (and perhaps considering throwing out this book as well!). But you must not allow the enormity of our goal to discourage or overwhelm you. The weed springs up quickly and is gone in a season, but the mighty oak slowly and deeply sends forth its roots, and after years of steady growth, rises to majestic heights. Mighty men, like mighty oaks, do not spring forth in a day or even a year; they are grown over the years of a lifetime.

Some victories and attainments will come easily and quickly, but others will come more slowly. At times we will face weaknesses within ourselves that seem the habitation of seven demons. Changes in these areas will only come after days, weeks, months and years of working and waiting. They will come as a result of prayer, fasting and intense Bible study, with the help of other men and after the hard disciplines of suffering, frustration and failure. We must understand that these challenges are a natural and indispensable part of the training and growth that it takes to become a mighty man.

I have been a disciple for more than thirty years. I began my quest as a nineteen-year-old teenager. When I made that decision, I did not know all that was ahead of me, but only *who* was ahead of me. And although I grew and changed over the years, there were some flaws in my character that seemed impossible to overcome. Sometimes, as I have looked back on my life months and years later, I have realized that somewhere along the way a great change has finally occurred—without my realizing exactly when! Some of the greatest changes in my life have occurred in the last few months, growth which I have sought for years. I have had to learn that the transformation of character is a lifetime development, and while I cannot stop passionately pursuing the goal, I must patiently accept and even embrace the process.

There is in the last verse of Isaiah chapter forty a beautiful description of the way God works in our lives. We are told there that sometimes we fly, sometimes we run, and at other times we walk. When we soar as an eagle, it seems as if we can glide freely in the heavens, gazing down with a serene and laughing heart at the weaknesses and problems that once bound us to earth. When we run with the effortless grace and speed of a thoroughbred, we traverse vast distances and leave our sins and difficulties in the dust behind us. And then there are the times when we proceed with the slow, measured tread of a walking man. We plod ahead with progress painfully slow, with our eyes fixed wistfully upon the goal we wish to one day attain.

While we all long to soar like the eagle and run like the racehorse, we must realize that most of life's progress is made as we walk faithfully forward. When God allows you to soar and to run, then fly as high and run as fast and as far as you can. But when he bids you to walk, then walk on, no matter how slow your progress may seem. Walk patiently, courageously, unflinchingly forward, and never, never turn back.

Following a man like Jesus will not be easy, and the victories will not be given us cheaply. Along the way, we will have amazing conquests and crushing defeats. But let us never forget the words of Solomon: "for though a righteous man falls seven times, he rises again" (Proverbs 24:16). One day all the years of striving, praying, repenting and believing will finally come to fruition. One day we will lay down our armor and be at rest. On that day we who are righteous will indeed rise again—to our final destination. On that day we will see Jesus with eyes unfettered by sin, unbelief and selfishness. On that day we will see him as he is, and we will be like him. On that day we will receive at last our crown of glory.

Until that day, let us never give up the fight. Let us rise to the challenge, and delight in the glory of seeing our lives transform day after day, year after year. And as we go, let us always remember that a mighty man is not a man who never suffers defeat but is one who refuses to remain defeated. Let these words, spoken by one of the greatest dreamers in literature, Don Quixote de la Mancha, be our heart's inspiration and our soul's theme:

To dream the impossible dream,
To fight the unbeatable foe,
To bear with unbearable sorrow,
To run where the brave dare not go

To right the unrightable wrong,
To love pure and chaste from afar,
To try, when your arms are too weary,
To reach the unreachable star.

This is my quest, to follow that star,
No matter how hopeless, no matter how far,
To fight for the right, without question or pause,
To be willing to march into hell for a heavenly cause,
And I know if I'll only be true to this glorious quest

That my heart will lie peaceful and calm when I'm laid to
   my rest.

And the world will be better for this,
That one man, scorned and covered with scars,
Still strove with his last ounce of courage
To reach the unreachable star!*

*"The Impossible Dream (The Quest)" from *Man of La Mancha.* Music by
Mitch Leigh. Lyrics by Joe Darion. Original American cast, UNI/MCA, 1973.

ADVENTURES, ACCOMPLISHMENTS AND EXPLOITS

Benaiah...was a valiant fighter...who performed great exploits.

2 Samuel 23:20

I began this book with a letter I sent out to a small group of men in the Triangle Church, our own group of Mighty Men. The goal of the group is simple: to imitate the heart and deeds of David's mighty men, who were the most valiant, skilled and passionate warriors of their time. At the first meeting of this group, I laid out seven areas in which the mighty men should grow and excel: spirituality, family life, career, finances, benevolence, physical fitness and fruitfulness. Each man left that first meeting and made goals for himself in each of the seven areas.

When any member of the Mighty Man group sets himself apart as one who has achieved stellar progress in his goals, he is awarded his Mighty Man Sword, an award to treasure for a lifetime. This sword is only given to those who have set themselves apart as men worthy of respect and honor in all areas of their lives, men who can truly be called *mighty.*

While only a small number of men have thus far received their swords, the accomplishments of the entire group since its establishment in August 1997 have been astounding. These men are men just like you: some are young and some are old; some single and some married; some are students, some blue-collar workers and others white-collar workers; some are ministers on staff; others are strong members of the congregation; they are men of all races and backgrounds. The only thing that sets them apart from other men is that they have chosen to challenge themselves and one another to take their spirituality and their lives higher than many ever dreamed they could.

In the spirit of 2 Samuel 23, in which the Bible lists the noteworthy feats of David's mighty men, I include here the accomplishments thus far achieved by the Triangle Mighty Men. Some of their victories may seem small, others are glorious. I list these achievements not to boast about these men (although I am extremely proud of them), but rather to give God glory for the work he has done in their lives. Each Mighty Man knows without a doubt that anything great he has done has been solely by the grace of God working powerfully in his life. Many of these men set goals they feared were unattainable, dreams they feared unreachable—but in a short time God has allowed them to achieve the "impossible" in their lives. It is my earnest desire that reading the extraordinary accomplishments of ordinary men will inspire you to know that you too can become a mighty man of God. May this list start you dreaming and aspiring, so that soon you can praise God for your own mighty deeds.

Mitch Mitchell: He serves as the leader of the Mighty Man group and my righthand in leading the Triangle Church. He leads camping and hiking trips six to eight times per year to mentor, inspire and challenge other Mighty Men. He and his wife, Jan, have baptized both of their children, Joshua (17) and Jessica (14). He has led two Triangle Church Bible Jubilees in 1998. He ran over 1,800 miles in 18 months and maintained a 25 pound weight loss. He ran 100 holes of golf during a HOPE gold tournament (a distance exceeding 26 miles) and has lowered his golf handicap from 13 to seven in the past two years. He started a "Y2K20" discipling group for those over forty to build leadership among the older marrieds in the church. *Mitch received his Mighty Man sword on March 8, 1998.*

Art Belden: He raised $9,000 for the HOPE Golf Tournament. As a newer disciple, he has already turned his marriage around and made tremendous strides in raising his children. As a man over 50, Art is one of the two oldest Mighty Men. He is Triangle Church's largest and most generous giver for its annual missions contribution. He raised $45,000 for HOPE Worldwide from corporate sources and set up new financial arrangements for Triangle Church's building and grounds improvements. He served on the Triangle Church Board of Directors for 1997-1998. *Art received his Mighty Man sword on March 8, 1998.*

Dr. Estrada Bernard: He is an eight-year member of the Triangle Church. He was recently appointed to the rank of Van L. Weatherspoon Associate Professor of Neurosurgery, an endowed Chair at the University of North Carolina School of Medicine, one of only 125 African Americans who currently hold such appointments; he received this honor at the age of 38, the youngest doctor ever to be so recognized in the field of neurosurgery. He was the first of only two African Americans trained in neurosurgery at Duke University. He received a successful review of his Neurosurgery Residency Training Program with full accreditation in 1998. He does 95 push-ups three times a week and finished the 1998 Triangle Fall Festival 5K race at a seven-minute mile pace; in this race, Estrada achieved the Herculean achievement of defeating Sam Laing, a goal he set after his previous loss in 1997 to this much older man. *Estrada received his Mighty Man sword on October 10, 1998.*

Tony Lewis: He has successfully completed two marathons: the 1997 Jacksonville Marathon, and the 1998 Kiawah Island Marathon. He has completed over 10 triathlons in the last three years with a personal record of 1:22. He leads the largest region of the Triangle Church and preached his first sermon before the entire congregation in 1998. His wife, Paige, also completed her first marathon this past fall. *Tony received his Mighty Man sword on October 10, 1998.*

Kevin Thompson: Kevin will graduate from Duke University in the fall of 1999 after five seasons as a full-scholarship football player. He recently made the Dean's List and raised his GPA to above 3.0. He led to Christ his friend Eric Jones, a starting free safety and captain on the Duke football team. He started an Ironman group to raise up leaders in the campus ministry. Under his leadership the Duke ministry has grown from two to 13. He preached his first sermon to a crowd of 150 in the Duke University student center. He set a goal to bench-press 350 pounds and now benches 360 and completed a triathlon this spring. He proposed marriage to Elizabeth Laing (my wonderful, incredible, brilliant, talented daughter) and they were married on May 22, 1999. Kevin and Elizabeth will remain in Durham where Kevin will play his last season as one of the quarterbacks on the Duke University football team, and Elizabeth will serve on the staff of our campus ministry. After the fall they plan to move to Atlanta, Georgia, to work in the campus ministry there. *Kevin was awarded his Mighty Man sword in April, 1999.*

Dr. Kevin Broyles: He organized the 1998 HOPE for Kids rally and raised over $100,000 for HOPE in 1996. At age 40, he became the Medical Director for a new initiative to create an urgent-care system at Duke University Medical Center, which became profitable after only three months of operation. He brought more than 20 visitors with him to the Triangle Church medical ministry's Bring Your Neighbor Day service in the fall of 1998. He served as the president for the local Board of Directors for HOPE for five years. He has volunteered regularly for the HOPE homeless shelter for the past seven years. He and his wife Noelle have increased their regular and missions contributions every year for the past 10 years. At the age of 41, he is now in better shape physically than he was at age 30.

Casto Fernandez: Casto excelled in a public speaking course at UNC-Chapel Hill and has become a powerful preacher. Under his leadership in 1998, the campus ministry led the church in net growth (44%) and in giving for the missions contribution. In 1999 the campus ministry held its first worship service ever on the campus of Duke University. He has memorized large portions of Romans, six different Psalms, and parts of Galatians, Philippians and 2 Timothy. He has raised up 13 new students into leadership roles in the campus ministry in 1998. He is one of the most physically fit of the Mighty Men, excelling in running, weightlifting and dance ability. He and his wife Angie are accomplished dance instructors.

Kevin Darby: Kevin, the music director of Triangle Church, produced, arranged and recorded a new CD, *Be Still, My Soul*, in half the normal time of putting out an album. He wrote two new songs in 1997 and one new song in 1998. He was hired to be the musical director for the Durham Arts Council's "Dance Kaleidoscope," a special outreach program to get inner-city and underprivileged children involved in the arts. He serves as the director of Triangle Church's annual Christmas production, *A Little Christmas Spirit*, which for the last two years was voted "Best Local Theater Production" in the Triangle area by *Spectator* magazine. He continues to develop the church's Web site, *trianglechurch.com,* and has received recognition for keeping it actively updated and relevant. He has significantly lowered his cholesterol level with a disciplined diet and regular exercise.

Kurt Dixon: His greatest accomplishment is the radical turnaround of his marriage—he and his wife had been separated and divorce was looming, but their relationship has now been restored and continues to grow. He is a US Naval Academy graduate and former Captain in the Marines who completed the 1998 Marine Corps Marathon. Currently an attorney, Kurt completed the first trial in which he was appointed lead counsel.

Arthur Grayson: Arthur and his wife, Elizabeth, led the Chapel Hill/Medical ministries of the Triangle Church to more than 30% growth in 1998. He has lost 55 pounds and has learned to play golf, consistently shooting in the 80s. He is currently learning first-year, college level Greek. He has dramatically changed in his marriage and is striving to be an awesome husband to his wife and father to his two daughters.

Dr. George Hill: He completed his foot and ankle surgical residency at the New York College of Podiatric Medicine and Affiliated Hospitals in 1991—only one of four African Americans in the United States to complete a foot and ankle surgical residency that year. He opened his own private office of podiatry, which has become profitable after its first year. He established a foot-screening clinic for the poor at Lincoln Community Health Center in Durham. He is the first podiatrist to work in a wound clinic in the division of vascular surgery at the University of North Carolina and the first African American podiatrist to work at UNC.

David Hawkins: He has recently baptized a friend into Christ and has powerfully led the Durham/Chapel Hill teen ministry of the Triangle Church, a group that saw 70% growth in 1998 from 30 to 50-plus teenagers. David recently celebrated reaching his seventh drug-free year and serves as the leader of the church's Chemical Recovery group. He reenrolled in North Carolina Central University with a double major in criminal justice and psychology and will graduate this summer with a college GPA of 3.6, doubling his high-school GPA of 1.8.

Tim Hoegemeyer: Tim has done a tremendous job leading the Raleigh/Cary teen ministry while working full-time with a new job at BB&T Bank. As a former Marine lieutenant, Tim is setting up a network of communication for disciples who are sent away on active duty in the military. In 1998 he eliminated all his debt, married his wife, Jennifer, and purchased his first home.

Tex Law: Tex serves the Triangle Church as its outstanding property manager. In 1998 he headed up the construction of a new pavilion and recording studio and also organized crews from Triangle Church to help with the construction of the Atlanta Church of Christ's summer camp. He has been drug-free for five years and helps to lead the Chemical Recovery ministry. Two of his daughters, Sarah (16) and Emily (14), have become disciples.

Phil Millis: Phil has made amazing changes in a marriage and family that were on the verge of disintegration. He has maintained a 20 pound weight loss. He completed the restoration and painting of a widow's home in 1998. He recently planned and oversaw a major renovation of the Triangle Church's grounds. At the age of 45, Phil has started a new career and begun course work to further his professional goals.

Rick Overturf: Rick has organized an ongoing auto repair project to help single mothers, single women and the needy, in which he and other brothers in the church have completed over $17,000 worth of labor for free. He has put in many hours of labor attempting to salvage the Laings' 1984 Jeep Cherokee as it struggled for survival. He has memorized over 100 new Bible verses. He and his wife, Lynn, have led the Raleigh sector of Triangle Church to a great turnaround and amazing growth. Rick has gotten his family completely out of debt.

Dr. Tom Perkins, M.D., Ph.D: Tom passed the national board exam for neurology, completed his residency at Duke and began private practice. He has developed a new sleep laboratory for his practice, which has already become successful. He memorized the entire book of James. He has successfully completed his first half-marathon last year, dropped his 5K time in 1998 and managed to defeat Sam Laing in the Triangle Fall Festival 5K, a much older man who had beaten him soundly the year before.

Greg Reiter: Greg has helped countless singles in the church with their finances and careers and has now helped more than 10 people to become debt-free. He gave over 25% of his income, including his missions contribution, to God in 1998. His USVA volleyball team finished fifth in the state, and his local basketball team won the championship game two seasons in a row. He and his wife now lead the Raleigh/Cary singles while he works full-time for Nortel. He helped with the church's tax workshop in February 1999 and recently purchased a new home to help the ministry in Cary.

Kevin Stewman: Kevin took over the job of financial administrator at Triangle Church. Under his leadership, the church received a stellar auditor's report in 1998. He organized a tax workshop and legal cafeteria (in which the attorneys in the congregation offered free legal help) for the church in 1999. He personally provides free legal services to church members who need his help but cannot afford an attorney. He serves as a member of the Triangle Church Board of Directors.

Dr. Bill Thompson, M.D., MBA: In 1998 he produced a feature film and raised over half a million dollars for its production. At age 55, he is the oldest member of the Mighty Men. He began a new career path involving two managed care systems in North Carolina and several physicians' practices. He will begin managing a number of physician malpractice companies within two years. He helped initiate the Mighty Man group's "Joseph Project," which assists single men with their careers, finances and dreams. He is an avid backpacker who led other Mighty Men on a 13 mile hike and campout on the coldest day and night of December 1998. He met and conquered the challenge of prostate cancer in August 1998. He has lost twelve pounds and is in his best physical shape in five years.

Rick Wallace: As a former sub-four-minute miler at North Carolina State University, Rick has reclaimed his running career: he has dropped two minutes off his 5K time and last year ran his first marathon in 3:30. He began the Triangle Running Club, which has over 100 members and sponsored its second annual 5K race in September 1998, with over 700 participants. He has also maintained an 18 pound weight loss. Rick recently made a career change that may result in a fifty-percent salary increase this year.

Ben Weast: He memorized and publicly recited the book of Philippians, a performance in which he portrayed the apostle Paul. He and his wife, Beth, lead the Triangle Church's Children's Ministry, and he has created a "Big Brother" program for middle schoolers without fathers. He has helped to coordinate and write for the Kingdom Kids Curriculum, a series of lessons for use in children's ministry around the world and also contributed many devotionals to *As For Me and My House,* a book of devotionals for families. He and his wife have helped many families in the Triangle Church to become more spiritual, godly and unified. He baptized his next-door neighbors.

John York: As the radical-in-residence of the Mighty Men, John is often compared to David's mighty man Benaiah. A former Marine sergeant, he ran the Marine Corps Marathon in the fall of 1998. He has maintained a 25 pound weight loss goal and successfully climbed a 5.8 sheer rock wall. He and his wife, Diana, are officially certified with the Hospice of North Carolina. He has completed 2,200 pages of study toward his goal of an in-depth study of the entire New Testament. He has had six or more visitors to church every Sunday of 1999.

Armor-Bearers

David Laing: As an 18-year-old high school senior, David is an armor-bearer for the Mighty Man group—a Mighty Man in training. He memorized the book of 2 Timothy in 1998. David played the lead male role in his high school's production of *West Side Story.* He ran a personal record 17:30 in a 5K race in the fall. He participated in a 13 mile mountain hike in December 1998. He was the North Carolina winner in the Sons of the American Revolution oratorical contest and will travel to

San Diego for the national competition this summer. He won two "Best Attorney" awards at the regional Mock Trial competition. He was awarded "most likely to succeed" and "most intellectual" senior superlatives. He was given the John Milton Award for senior English composition. He finished his senior year with a straight A average. He has received scholarship offers from two well-known universities. He is currently organizing a teen/preteen mentoring project called the "Joshua Project." He serves as the leader of the teen ministry of his high school, a ministry that recently baptized three students in one week.

Jonathan Laing: Jonathan, also an armor-bearer in the Mighty Man group is, at age 16, the youngest member. He played a strong supporting role in *West Side Story*. He completed his sophomore year of high school with a straight A average. He has increased his bench press weight over 45 pounds. He ran a PR 18:27 in a 5K race and once ran 15 miles while training for his school's cross-country team. He participated in a 13 mile hike in December 1998. He memorized the book of 2 Timothy in 1998. For three years, he played a major role in Triangle Church's award winning production of *A Little Christmas Spirit.*

There are also three new members of the Mighty Men for 1999: Wayne Smith, Jim Kitchen and Farad Ali, who are currently in the process of attaining their goals.

These adventures, accomplishments and exploits speak for themselves. I hope they inspire you to dream, to aspire and to do your own mighty deeds!

Who Are We?

Discipleship Publications International (DPI) began publishing in 1993. We are a nonprofit Christian publisher affiliated with the International Churches of Christ, committed to publishing and distributing materials that honor God, lift up Jesus Christ and show how his message practically applies to all areas of life. We have a deep conviction that no one changes life like Jesus and that the implementation of his teaching will revolutionize any life, any marriage, any family and any singles household.

Since our beginning we have published more than 75 titles; plus we have produced a number of important, spiritual audio products. More than one million volumes have been printed, and our works have been translated into more than a dozen languages—international is not just a part of our name! Our books are shipped regularly to every inhabited continent.

To see a more detailed description of our works, find us on the World Wide Web at **www.dpibooks.com.** You can order books by calling 1-888-DPI-BOOK twenty-four hours a day. From outside the US, call 781-937-3883, ext. 231 during Boston-area business hours.

We appreciate the hundreds of comments we have received from readers. We would love to hear from you. Here are other ways to get in touch:

Mail: DPI, One Merrill St., Woburn, MA 01801
E-mail: dpibooks@icoc.org

Find us on the World Wide Web

www.dpibooks.com
1-888-DPI-BOOK
outside US: 781-937-3883 x231